# THROUGH THE DESERT TO THE GRASSY PLAIN

## THE SPIRITUAL AUTOBIOGRAPHY OF AN ORDINARY SPECIAL PERSON

## BY RODGER TUTT (TED JONES)

# TABLE OF CONTENTS

# INTRODUCTION

Are you satisfied with evangelicalism, or has it caused you more problems than it has solved. If evangelicalism has been more of a burden than a help to you then this book is for you.

After 28 years of futile struggling to embrace evangelicalism and make it his own, the author has obtained a measure of hope that is changing his life for the better.

Although this book doesn't offer a "know for sure" philosophy like the evangelicals have, it is the author's humble prayer that it might be used to help other struggling souls through this veil of tears called life.

The hope that the author has acquired has been powerful enough to begin changing him from a neurotic puppet, into a happy individual who has the highest regard both for himself and for every other person that God has created.

We all still have a long way to go, but be patient; God is not finished with us yet.

# ABOUT THE TITLE

I chose the title THROUGH THE DESERT TO THE GRASSY PLAIN because the comparative freedom from emotional conflict and pain of my last two years is such a great contrast to the inner frustration and pain of my first thirty-eight years. I have passed through the barren desert of evangelicalism to the grassy plain of agnosticism.

Other titles that I considered appropriate were

A SPIRITUAL AUTOBIOGRAPHY

THE STRUGGLES OF A DESPERATE SOUL

THIS IS ME! FOLKS

COMING TO GRIPS WITH LIFE

A BILL OF DIVORCE

THE TYRANNY OF EVANGELICALISM

HOW I ESCAPED FROM EVANGELICALISM

"WHY" AND "HOW" I BECAME AN AGNOSTIC

and lastly, an addition to the Moody Press series:

DOCTRINE OF DEVILS – EVANGELICALISM

No tongue-in-cheek facetiousness is intended by this title. I am completely serious about it. It is my opinion that there is as much, or more, "devil doctrine" in evangelicalism as there is in any other theology that claims to be pro-God.

The important difference between evangelicals and myself is that the love of my God includes devils.

Sure it's true that I only have <u>hope</u> in my concept of God, but as I say several times in my book, "I'd rather have <u>hope</u> in my concept of God, than <u>faith</u> in the evangelical concept of God."

# DEDICATION

I dedicate this book to my son Steve and my daughter Beth, praying to God that it will help you both find <u>hope</u> in a concept of God that will enable you to successfully cope with all of life's problems.

If there ever comes a time that you feel that life is no longer worth living, I hope that you will read this book then, for I believe that somewhere in its pages you will find the spark that will motivate you to keep going.

I am deeply grateful to Miss Edith Blowing who read this manuscript through several times. As one of the few remaining "Christians" for whom I have any respect left, she has been an invaluable source of emotional strength through an extremely difficult period of time in my life. As a Christian, her attitude towards me, an agnostic, is almost unique within my own experience. Her attitude towards me keeps my hope alive that I may yet some time in the future, during this life time, be able to enjoy the fellowship of at least a few "Christians". The fact is that, at the present, I experience a high degree of emotional pain when I am with any of my "Christian" associates of the past. I'm afraid I know them all too well. To ask them to react towards me like Miss Blowing does is asking for a miracle. As an agnostic, I can only <u>hope</u> that it might happen. I know that Christians <u>believe</u> in miracles, but I'm not sure that any "Christian" I know would even <u>want</u> to experience the miracle of being able to be tolerant towards a self confessed agnostic.

I also dedicate this book to my father and my three brothers, and to Eric & Jean Beyers who have all been a help and encouragement to me.

Most of all, I dedicate it to my wife who means more to me than I can put into words. In order to properly pay tribute to her, I would need to write a book as lengthy as this one already is. I am so grateful to God for allowing her to be part of my life!

# FOREWARD

Traveling with Roger through his DESERT JOURNEY and GRASSY PLAINS has been for me a unique experience.

There has never been a time in his life when he has not been very precious to me, and yet there was a side of his life and thinking that I was completely unaware of. Not until it was my privilege to read this documentary was I made aware of just how much harm some of our so-called "fundamental" teachings can do. To have watched, and I might add watched carefully and prayerfully, a life emerge from fear and self-guilt to one of hope and complete love has been thrilling.

If, for no other reason that someone who holds the "doctrine of salvation through fear of punishment" as "sound" doctrine, would come to see God of Love as Roger has, and the hope which he now has through all his times of stress and hurt is the way of eternal life, then his work, and the pain which he has suffered in revealing his innermost self, will have been very worthwhile.

Even some of Roger's critics who have so bitterly condemned him, would benefit greatly from his story, if they would prayerfully consider what harm can be done to a soul that is not regarded with love and respect when trying to set themselves up as one with God to judge a fellow man, and ask what can be done for that soul to show God in His Infinite Love and Wisdom.

Thank you Roger, for letting me express what I feel about a piece of reading that would be beneficial to not only those who criticize but could also help others who are struggling with some of the same problems that you faced, to find their "Grassy Plain".

Edith M. Blowing

# PREFACE

In order to keep the emotions and attitudes manifested in this book, both by myself and others, in their proper perspective, it is important at the outset that I address myself to two particular questions that have been asked about me.

1. Why does Roger keep saying that we think a certain way when he really doesn't know what we think?

2. Why won't Roger realize that organizations and individuals within those organizations may have changed?

In answer to the first question, the reader needs to realize that this book is a record of my reactions to my contacts with endless hell people in various places, not just in one city. If the statement doesn't apply to you then ignore it, because it was not meant for you.

It is important to recognize that I'M NOT NECESSARILY ATTACKING WHAT YOU MEANT, BUT RATHER I'M ATTACKING WHAT I THINK YOU MEANT. In other words, I'm not reacting to individuals, but I am reacting to attitudes and beliefs WHETHER OR NOT I HAVE

CORRECTLY ASCRIBED THEM TO THE PERSON IN QUESTION.

It is not my intention that this book should be taken personally. It is for this reason that I have made certain persons anonymous. If you don't take it personally, you won't be hurt by it. If my understanding of your attitude or any of your statements has hurt you, I apologize.

In answer to the second question, it is important to keep in mind that it has taken me years to write this book. My attitudes and emotions have mellowed and changed too. Many of the attitudes and emotions that I express herein, may not be a valid description of the state of my soul and spirit by the time you read this book.

Certain evangelicals who read my book may question the accuracy of the quotes that I have attributed to them, or at least may claim that I have misinterpreted what they have said. They may also maintain that I am not sensitive to the possibility that my "misquotes" or "misinterpretations" may hurt some people's feelings.

If they say these things they will have missed the only REALLY IMPORTANT ISSUE in my book.

I could have spent time substantiating the accuracy of my quotes. For example, my former Bible school class mates might say, "I don't remember a teacher saying that if a person led a Godly life, but at the end of his life he renounced Christ, he would go to endless hell." I could have refreshed their memory by saying that the teacher's statement was made after he told the story about the "Christians" who were forced to stand on a frozen lake in the nude. One "Christian" renounced Christ and ran to shore to save his life, while a heathen on the shore took off his clothes and ran out to die with the Christians.

I could have substantiated other quotes this way, but I would have been detouring from the only really important reason for writing this book.

To the best of my knowledge I have not misquoted anyone, nor have I intentionally misinterpreted anything that anyone has said. But all this is beside the point.

Let's suppose, for the sake of getting my point across, that my whole book is a pack of deliberate lies, and that I invented all the evidences and all the quotes that support my concept of God. THE POINT IS, WHAT THEN?!

Suppose the motivation for my writing this book were totally corrupt. WHAT THEN?! Would God allow me to want to suffer endlessly rather than submit to Him, or would He successfully bring influence to bear upon my will to convince me that the way I had chosen was wrong?

Evangelicals who take the time to argue about the accuracy of my quotes, or the validity of my interpretation of what has been said to me by them, are missing the only really important purpose for writing this book.

In a way, I couldn't care less if the quotes are inaccurate, or if I have misinterpreted what the evangelicals have said, or even if I have hurt people's feelings. The only thing that's important to me is, WHAT'S GOD GOING TO DO ABOUT IT? Is He going to let me wind up in endless suffering because of it, or is He going to smarten me up so I'll want to come to Him to be changed?

Evangelicals will answer, "That's up to you." And my reply is, "Now we are down to the only really important issue; It's not up to me, IT'S UP TO GOD!

The only really important thing in this whole book is THE ABSOLUTE SOVEREIGNTY OF GOD OVER THE SALVATION OF EVERY SOUL!!!

As Ray Prinzing puts it, "The journey away from and the journey back to God are both under His sovereign control. The end is secure for everyone!"

# NO ONE IS GOING TO
# SUFFER ENDLESSLY

A small section at the front of this book is entitled A DESERT JOURNEY. It was written during several long sleepless nights. It marks the end of my "desert journey" through evangelicalism, and the beginning of my comparatively pleasant journey over the GRASSY PLAIN of agnosticism. It was written several months before I started writing the main bulk of my book which is entitled THE GRASSY PLAIN. A DESERT JOURNEY is not pleasant reading. It describes the suffering of a desperate, tormented soul who managed to survive the first thirty years of his life by clinging desperately to a fragile thread of hope, the hope that God was not really like the evangelicals said He was.

Gordon Sinclair is probably Toronto's best known atheist. "any times, when I was an evangelical, I listened to other evangelicals speak words of vicious condemnation of this man. Ever did I hear words of compassionate concern."

I commend the United Church of Canada "ANLATR" for publishing his honest doubts.

Another public figure that has suffered the same intensity of abuse by the evangelicals is Charles Templeton who was once an evangelist with the Billy Graham Crusade, but who, because of honest doubts, now publicly declares himself to be agnostic.

With the exception of the doctrine of endless hell, the questions that bother these men are not a problem to me. My concept of how the Bible reveals God and His plan takes care of all that.

I believe it will be better for every created being that every negative thing happened to them. God will not just "make it up to them," but he will see to it that it will be better that each negative thing happened than had it not happened, and this includes Satan!

However, I find myself in a common bond of kinship with these two fine gentlemen; for I, like they, have suffered the same kind of "it's us and God against you" attitude from my evangelical friends, because of my rejection of the belief that the Bible teaches that there is an endless hell.

I am hoping my book, THROUGH THE DESERT TO THE GRASSY PLAIN, will cause some of my evangelical friends to re-examine their attitude to those of us who have "honest doubts".

I am afraid that my faith in the idea that such a miracle as this might actually happen during this lifetime, is overpowered by the strength of the numerous negative reactions that I have experienced in the past.

Yet I know in my heart that even this negative situation will work out better that it happened that way.

# A TRIBUTE TO MY FATHERS WORK

by Steven Tutt (Jones)

Rodger Tutt has taken it upon himself to address and confront one of the central ideas of many Christians and of one most misused and misdirected tools of Christianity; that of controlling people through the fear of endless hell.

His heart-felt knowing of God let him ask something like - If God Loves us, and is omnipotent, how could/would God determine that any being suffering endlessly would/could serve Loves purpose?

Even with the imposed threat of his eternal damnation looming over his head, his spirit could not accept this distortion of Gods Love

He was taught that even to question the teachings, or consider another perspective was a sin. He had to swallow and believe everything he was told, no questions. This type of "fear-control" of a persons free thought and freedom to consider and evaluate other options is a very destructive, controlling, and blatant misuse of mind control and manipulation.

Even with no one else to back him up and no other alternative idea to comfort him, he knew, if only through its absence that there was another way. So he set out into the emptiness of total blind faith, alone, with no map, and no cane, only the pure faith and knowing that God is Love, to find the description or view of God that gave the true picture of a loving God.

I'm sure if you ask him he will tell you something like " he had no faith or knowing that God was Love at all, and that he had a nervous breakdown, and could only hope there was a better way".

But his inability to accept that a loving God would let any being suffer forever shows me that even though he had no words to describe what he felt, he knew this was not the way of Love or a loving God. Nervous Breakdown, whatever, call it what you will. I think it was the true loving God taking hold of him in the only language he had been taught, fear. I think it said to him in a voice he only could hear inside himself, something like:

"This that you call a nervous breakdown, is my loving hands stopping you from a life lived in fear.

Those that you love will damn you, as those that I loved betrayed me. But they do not know me as you do, they think I am a cruel God, but even though you have no words to protest your heart knows me and knows that I am a God of Love.

You may not understand what I am doing in your mind, or know that this fear is my hands loving you, because I talk to you with the grip of fear, and deep inside you know I am love. But, know in your soul where you have not words for it, that when this fear passes you will be free to live in the knowing of my Love.

Know that none will need to suffer forever, or even for a moment more than must be. Those who damn you are damning themselves to a life lived in fear, for they choose to believe that their God would allow a being to suffer eternal extreme cruelty with nothing good ever coming from it. In their minds they live in a world which is ruled by a cruel God.

When they are drawing their final breaths they may still believe they are being delivered into such cruel hands. They will not live in the peace knowing of my unconditional Love until they accept that none will be lost, none will be left behind.

I am assisting you through this temporary fear for it stops you from swallowing the poison of accepting that I am a cruel God. Here I set you free. I set free to find the way of my love which is unconditional, and if one loves without condition, none can be turned away."

Rodgers experience was of terror, immobilizing, paralyzing. He did not have the comfort of realizing what was said to him at the time. But he went on anyway, and searched as in the dark for people with other answers, as one would search for needles in a haystack. The people-needles would help him burst the bubbles of illusion and fear people had blown into his brain. In time he found these people amongst the billions that live on this earth and from each he took and preserved each little needle they gave and from them he fashioned a sword of truth, a sword of Love and Light that he would use to cut away the bonds of control, fear and guilt from others, and let them see the Love of God.

Someone had to make the sword, and working metal is a hot and tiresome job. The sword had to be very strong. Much time was needed to be put into its making. Its strength had to be of the highest integrity, so many tests were put upon it.

Rodger Tutt was commissioned by God to make this sword. He is his own testament to himself that everything will be better that it happened. For if he did not go through what he did he would never have known how the sword must be made or had the persistence to see its completion.

His spirit is the essence of the sword.

The words of his book, the actions of his life, his thoughts and speech, make up the blade.

When I was growing up I remember hearing the forging of that sword. For many hours of many days, behind the door of his sword making shop that he called his room, I heard him forming its shape and perfecting the details on the forge he called his typewriter. I hear he still sits sharpening his sword.

He is generous in letting others use it.

He has an ad in the paper that offers the sword to people who need it. That they might have their bindings of illusion and fear removed, and be shown the true loving God.

His ad simply says

"Hell is not endless, call Rodger Tutt 905-886-****"

You can leave a message there. He will get back to you, and I'm sure he will share the sword with you if you ask.

The proud son of a spiritual warrior called Rodger Tutt.

Steve P. Tutt (Jones)

# A DESERT JOURNEY

It was my intention to entitle what I have written, "EVAN-GELICAL TYRANNY," but through the hours that I have been putting my thoughts on paper, my bitterness began to be replaced with an inner strength. Consequently I now prefer to entitle my effort, "A DESERT JOURNEY".

If, or when I ever visit my endless hell friends again, I will refuse to discuss religion with them. I am not emotionally strong enough to do so. However I would be happy to correspond by mail with anyone who might like to discuss the contents herein.

The kingdom of Roger Tutt must and will sooner or later be destroyed. Your kingdom must be destroyed too, whether it be a personal kingdom or an organizational kingdom. It must be destroyed so that only the pure kingdom of God remains. Before you answer back that you do not have a kingdom that is not synonymous with the kingdom of God, I urge you to read this manuscript from beginning to end, and then see if you can still arrive at the same conclusion.

Right at the start I want to make the declaration that I want to be on God's side, and I renounce Satan and all his ways. I used to make this declaration periodically before my nervous breakdown ten years ago, but now in 1976 it takes on an entirely new significance. I don't want to go to an endless hell, but I know from past experience that some of my readers will conclude that that is exactly what is going to happen to me unless I repent of the attitude that I manifest in these my writings. For the sake of my sanity, or what's left of it, I must commit these people and their conclusions to God, and hope that he is not like they say He is.

The problem of the intensity of my suffering can be divided into two parts. The first part is an area beyond my control. It is the psycho neurotic phenomenon of just finding myself in a state of intense fear for no apparent reason. These spells sometimes last for days at a time. No day ever passes without suffering at least several hours of fear feelings for no apparent reason. Over the past ten years, both the intensity and the duration of these spells have been slowly decreasing. If I continue to improve over the next ten years at the same rate, I think that I might be able to cope with the crises of the death of my wife without being forced into suicide by being thrown back into the stark raving hideous terror that I experienced from 1966 to 68. Even now, if a normal person were able to live inside my skin on any given day, I'm sure they would be completely astounded as to how I can cope under the influence of the suffering that I endure day by day.

The second part of the problem of the intensity of my suffering has been caused by my uncontrollable reaction to the attempts of my endless hell friends to analyze my problems and offer what they consider to be a solution.

It's well known that it's not so much what people do to you that causes you to suffer; it's how you react to it. However, because I already suffer every day for no apparent reason, the fact that the "solutions" that my endless hell friends offer don't work causes them to condemn me for not making them work. It is this condemnation and my reaction to their statements of condemnation that is the basis of the second part of the problem of the intensity of my suffering.

Coupled with the second part of the problem of the intensity of my suffering is the added condemnation of the Scriptures. "God has not given us the spirit of fear, but of love, joy, and peace in the Holy Spirit", therefore I can't help but conclude that I do not have the Spirit of God. "God has given us the spirit of a sound mind," therefore I conclude that God doesn't love me, for He certainly hasn't given me a sound mind, and what is even more pertinent is that He hasn't even given me the ability to receive His Spirit of a sound mind.

I could go on and on demonstrating how the Scriptures condemn me rather than help me find an answer. This heavy weight of condemnation inflicted upon me both by my endless hell friends and the Scriptures, (Incidentally, "There is no condemnation to those who are in Christ Jesus", therefore I must not be in Christ Jesus), this heavy weight adds immeasurable intensity to the first part of my problem which is simply experiencing the emotion of fear for no apparent reason. When I try to stand back and look at myself objectively, I find it incredible that I am able to function at all in this life.

It has taken me ten years to accumulate sufficient emotional strength to face my problem head-on, and bring the intimate details out into the open where they can be seen clearly.

During the first few years of my life, my father lost both my mother and his second wife at childbirth. My attempts to adjust to the different ideas of right and wrong imposed upon me by the various housekeepers who looked after me utterly failed. By the time Dad married for the third time, both he and I were in a state of hopeless frustration .

One day, at the age of seven, I was sitting on the cellar steps watching my father sift the ashes from our coal furnace. He said to me that it was possible to tell at an early age when a child had irreversibly chosen the path that leads to an endless hell, and it was clear to me that he thought I had chosen that path.

Added to this frightful assertion by my father was another incident that also took place during my seventh year. I was in a state of bitter frustration after having been punished for what seemed to me to be the millionth time. Weeping with a depth of grief far beyond my years I went to my parents bedroom and pled with them to help me find a solution to my inability to behave. Their answer was that I had to get "saved". I had tried to "get saved before but nothing happened. Something happened at that moment way down in the depths of my psyche that made me certain that God had given up on me. A year later my parents sent me to a foster home because they could no longer cope with my behavior.

When I was fourteen, I ran away from home for a few months, and during these months I experienced one half hour of stark raving insanity, when all the suppressed emotions of my seven year old incident overwhelmed me.

At the age of twenty-one at Bible school, I experienced three hours of the same thing. Then at the age of twenty-eight as a missionary, I went into a complete breakdown condition. The stark raving hideous intensity of the terror of this experience is impossible for the normal person to even begin to imagine because their defense mechanisms wouldn't allow them to try.

The suffering of this experience made it possible for me to try to keep believing in a God who allows any of His created beings to suffer endlessly. This change in theology became the means by which I have recovered to the degree of stability that I now enjoy, or rather endure.

No matter how hard I try to tell them otherwise, my endless hell friends keep confusing the issue and insist that my theological change is the cause of my problem, when in reality it has been the key to all the progress that I have made in solving my problem to this point in time. Trying to remain a loyal subject of the kingdom set up by the endless hell people, has produced only <u>death</u> in me. The only <u>life</u> that I have experienced during the last ten years has come to me as a result of placing my hope in an entirely different set of beliefs, and now I feel the time has come to declare it publicly.

My endless hell friends say that in order for me to be restored to favor with God I have to leave the option open that the sufferings of hell might indeed be without end. The fact that I am simply unable to do this, causes them to stand in condemnation of me, and say that I am in fact in a state of rebellion, for they insist that I simply <u>won't</u>. They have also tried to cast evil spirits out of me, and told me that I am deceived by Satan, and that I'm destined to slide downward into a life of gross sin. A few have even said that they will have to stand at the judgment and say,"I tried to tell you so", as they watch me being banished to an endless hell of torment.

As you may well imagine, the incredible force of these negative assertions have retarded the rate of my recovery.

Before I begin to explain my theological change in detail, I would like you to examine the following exchange of letters, and then ponder the thoughts expressed at the end of the letters.

An open letter from Roger Tutt to anyone who might be interested – February 1976

The main purpose of this letter is to solidify my thinking about my present spiritual condition. However, it occurred to me at the outset that some of my friends might be interested in reading it. A psychologist might say that my desire to have my friends read it is an indirect way of asking for help, and I think I would be inclined to agree with them.

I am attempting to write what I have to say as objectively as possible, without any attempt to protect my ego, and trying not to allow bitterness or self pity color my point of view.

Since my nervous breakdown in 1966, I have suffered from the emotion of fear every day, with varying intensity and varying lengths of time. The cause of my fear is my inability to believe that the sufferings of hell are without end.

In 1969, after seven years of service, I was asked to leave a missionary society after telling them that I could no longer try to believe that hell was endless.

Different statements came from different people in the Bible school from which I graduated, One said that it was a "dangerous error" not to believe that hell is without end. Another said that I must leave the question in God's hands, and if it turns out that hell is indeed without end, God will justify His action in allowing it to be so.

The fact is that I'm not able to leave it in God's hands. If hell is without end, then I have no love or affection toward God. I have no respect for Him. I am only able to respond to Him in a state of cringing terror. Certainly I will obey Him, but only because He has allowed me to be in hell during my nervous breakdown, and I know if I don't line up with His will he will put me back into that state without end.

Another person at the Bible school said, "Your problem is not that you <u>can't</u> believe that hell is without end, it's that you <u>won't</u> believe it." No other statement in my whole life has caused me so much emotional pain, because this was said by a person that I deeply respect. The statement is ever so wrong! It plunges me into a state of hopeless frustration every time I think about it.

I am fully aware that I shall have to give an account for all the words that I have written at the judgment seat of Christ.

Since I cannot be sure what God is like, I don't have any faith. I realize that without faith I cannot please God, but if God is like I hope He is, then this problem will only be temporary.

In my present condition I am only the death of my wife away from total insanity or suicide. Although I am learning to love my eight year old son and my seven year old daughter more every day, I seriously doubt that this love alone would be a strong enough incentive to want to live on if I lost Helen. Her love for me is the only influence that is presently preventing me from losing my sanity completely or ending my life by my own hand.

A ray of hope has been shed into my life recently by the fact that my own father, who once said he believed I was part of Satan's Babalonian church, has now become solidly converted to belief in the total restoration of all.

I also have another source of hope.

For several years now I have been reading two periodicals, one the SPIRIT OF THE WORD, by Ed Gregory, and the other, GOSPEL ECHOES by Ray Prinzing; and recently I have been listening to a series of tapes by this same Prinzing.

Believe me, if God is like they say the Bible teaches He is, then there is plenty to really get excited about. Oh how strongly I hope he is really like that! If He is as they say the

Bible reveals He is, then there is absolutely nothing that I wouldn't try to endure for His sake with fullness of joy!

However, I see no future for myself other than to spend the rest of my life without joy or faith, because the endless hell people have too strong a hold on my mind and emotions. This is probably due to the fact that my disbelief in the endless sufferings of hell did not come about by examining objective evidences, but it was caused by the severity of suffering that I experienced during my nervous breakdown.

My nervous breakdown itself was caused by my inability to love or trust a god who would allow His created beings to suffer endlessly, and the intensity of the sufferings of my nervous breakdown has proven to be very much more powerful than many libraries full of objective evidence.

The sufferings of my nervous breakdown can quite accurately be compared to the descriptions of the sufferings of hell that are recorded in the Bible. To allow any being to stay in such a state and never get out of it would be totally useless and unnecessary, to say the least. The action is not worthy of any god who is seeking my loving allegiance.

There is a bright spot in my otherwise midnight sky and that is that I still have hope, not faith nor joy, just hope. It's not very strong hope, probably not strong enough to survive the death of my wife, but never the less I do have some hope. From an objective point of view, even the basis of my hope is not very secure looking. It is based on the interpretation of scripture as taught by a comparatively few people like Ed Gregory and Ray Prinzing. But my hope exists and it is real enough to keep me going.

The exposition of scripture based on the concept of the restoration of all is so breathtakingly wonderful that I wish with all my heart that the endless hell people could be open minded enough to at least consider it.

So this is 1976 and I press onward in living my life in hope, hope that God is not really like the endless hell people say He is. I live a very pathetic life, most of the time just glad that I was able to make it through another day.

However, if God is like I hope He is, He will one day take this very patheticness and even if necessary, my suicide and make something out of it for His glory.

The reader will probably conclude from this letter that I am emotionally sick or mentally ill, or both. This is probably true. I am hoping that God will help me find healing.

Before I close this letter I would like to relate an incredible story that I read about in the Montreal Star in 1965, a year before my nervous breakdown.

An Ohio lady, belonging to an endless hell section of the Christian church, had in 1959 drowned her two infants in a bathtub. She gave as her reason that she wanted to insure that her children would never have to suffer endlessly in hell. She was confined to a mental institution for two years and when she was released in 1962 she had two more children born to her in the following two years. She again drowned these in a bathtub giving the same reason.

In my judgment, from my point of view, this lady's act of "murder" was completely rational. What she did might not have been morally right according to the letter of the law, but her conclusion that God could not justly put her infants into an endless hell was certainly based on sound logic, unless of course you believe in inherited guilt.

This lady laid aside all concern for any consequences she herself might have to face for her acts of "murder" to insure her children a safe passage to heaven.

The only thing that prevents me from devising a scheme to destroy as many infants as possible is that I have, during my nervous breakdown, experienced the stark raving terror of hell and know that the several Biblical descriptions of hell can be experienced here in this life. I wouldn't deliberately do anything that might cause God to put me into such a state without end, not even to save the soul of my own wife.

I have just opened a letter that came today from a person who sent me more proof that hell is without end. This may only add more suffering to my life. I have already suffered so much from the words of the endless hell people. (Note: My fears about this "proof" turned out to be unwarranted.)

Sincerely yours in Christ (I hope)

Roger Tutt

Dear Roger:

Greetings in the name of our Saviour, Jesus Christ.

Thank you for sending me a copy of your open letter. I appreciate your openness in the things you said in it, even though I found much of it quite disturbing. It is worthwhile knowing your reasonings and having a glimpse of your present spiritual condition – though I am troubled to find you so disturbed.

I am sorry if my earlier letter to you, answering your request for light on the meaning of the Greek word aion, has only added more suffering to your life. As I write you now, I hope and pray that you will be able to accept these kindly intended words of council in the spirit in which they are given.

Remember the challenging words of Abraham: "Shall not the Judge of all the earth do right?" Whether or not I can comprehend what God is doing and satisfactorily understand His motives and methods, I know He will never do anything which is in any way wrong or which is not for the best. Why did He allow Adam and Eve to fall? Why does He allow heathen beliefs to persist, and atheism, Buddhism, Islam, and other errors? I can't comprehend why He didn't step in and undo all the human tangles of this world long ago. But just because He hasn't done things like I may think He should have doesn't mean that I know best and have the right to object to His actions or inactions. Should I find fault with God? Jesus addressed Him as "righteous Father." I also know on the authority of Jesus Himself, my

Savior that God is love, even though I can't always see this love. The fault is mine, not God's – my blindness and unresponsiveness are to blame, not any lack of care, kindness or grace on His part.

The Lord said to Moses, "I will have mercy on whom I will have mercy, and I will have compassion on whom I will have compassion." Why is this mercy and compassion not equally shown to everyone? – my logical mind asks. But who am I to find fault with God just because I cannot comprehend and understand all matters as He does. Any seeming contradiction between His righteousness and His love is the fault of my human perception. He fully proved His love in Jesus Christ, and my trust abides in Him. He is the anchor of my soul.

Whether hell for the lost be eternal or only short term, why should I let the matter disturb me? I am willing to allow God to do as He wishes, even if His actions should be contrary to what seems logical to my theology and human understanding.

Concerning the Ohio lady who thought she should kill her infants to save them from going to hell; she was clearly acting in rebellion to God's commandment, "Thou shalt not murder." She was acting on the assumption that she knew better than God. Did Jesus commission His disciples to go into all the world and save souls by killing infants? Whether or not her actions were rational – and I don't think they were – they clearly were not based on any command or scripture.

Really, it would be just as rational to murder infants and keep them from ever entering as adults into a short term hell as it would be to murder them to prevent their going to a long term hell. A short term hell theological view doesn't rationally solve the problem of living beyond the age of accountability. God knows what is best and has plainly said, "Thou shalt not kill." I'll accept His conclusions rather than hers. God is more rational than she (or you, or me).

And is it redundant for me to point out a fact you already know: that, "Thou shalt not kill" includes suicide?

Roger, you signed your open letter, "Sincerely yours in Christ (I hope). Don't let Satan cause you to doubt your being in Christ. You have for years trusted Christ as your Savior. Lack of assurance now in this matter of your salvation – any hope that is at a lower level than confidence – is clearly a fiery dart of the evil one. Put on the whole armour of God, and don't lay down the shield of faith in God's promises as found in His holy Word. This whole intellectual question concerning the duration of hell - and your inability to drop it into God's hands – is being used as a Satanic weapon against your faith in Christ. This whole outflow of the torrents of fear, sweeping against the foundation of your trust in God, is one of the wiles of the devil. There is no need for this state of mind to continue and bring you to another breakdown.

Fear is not one of the fruits of the Spirit. Nor is doubt. Don't let Satan gain the upper hand but be strong in the Lord and the power of His might. Jesus Christ already is victor and you are in Him. Count on it – count on Him. He is dependable even when we are not, even when we fail to wrestle against the powers of darkness. All things are possible through Christ who died to redeem you from all evil. Keep looking to Him, the strong one who now dwells within you. Remember, he suffered more for you than you have ever suffered and even your present sufferings are but the fellowship of His sufferings. He has made it possible for you to forget those things which are behind and press forward toward the mark for the prize of the high calling of God in Christ Jesus. Romans 8:28 is not an empty promise. Take Him as His word.

Look to Him and keep on keeping on in Christ.

In Him

    Bob


Note: This letter from Bob contained some positive statements of faith and encouraging words, but you will note from my reply that I disagreed strongly with some of the things he said.

Dear Bob:

Thank you for your letter of kindly intended words in response to my open letter.

In 1969 you offered to show me that I was wrong in not believing that hell never comes to an end. I refused your offer at the time because it would have been too emotionally painful to even consider any evidence that supported the idea of an endless hell. However, I have lived in constant fear as to what this evidence might be. I knew sooner or later that I would have to face up to it and ask you to tell me, which as you know I have done.

For the last ten years I have been examining all the reasons as to why I should not accept the interpretation of scripture as taught by the restoration people, and asking you for your evidence is part of the process of clearing my mind of the objections, and I am hoping that it will lead to being able to have faith, not just hope, in the ultimate restoration of every created being that continues to exist.

Your most recent letter convinces me that I was wise in postponing my dialogue with you, for after reading it, my body was actually numb for several hours from shock. I know that you were trying to be helpful and I have no bitter feelings towards you, but your letter revealed as almost total lack of understanding.

The hell that Jesus describes is a good description of what I went through during my nervous breakdown. A person would only have to be in it for a few short minutes before his attitude of rebellion against God would be completely reversed. To say that God gives the ability to a person to choose themselves into that state and will never, never let that stark raving hideous torment come to an end is making a veritable mockery out of the word "justice." My whole being screams within me that it cannot be – it just simply cannot be. There is absolutely nothing that anyone could do that would justify that kind of retribution without end!

Yes Bob, I <u>can</u> understand why God allowed Adam and Eve to fall, and Lucifer to rebel, and heathen beliefs and atheism, Buddhism, Islam and other "errors" to persist. I <u>can</u> understand why He hasn't stepped in to undo all the human tangles of this world.

If God is like I hope He is then the reason is simple. He restrains evil and only allows it to go as far as He wants it to in each individual. He knows exactly what He is going to do with each person, and he knows just how far to go in His rebellion, for He is going to use the experience gained in that very rebellion to one day work out for the person's own good and God's glory.

There is absolutely no comparison between questions like you asked above and the question of whether the sufferings of hell ever come to an end. The two subjects are an infinite distance apart. The questions that you posed above have no bearing whatsoever on whether or not God is just, loving and good like the question of an endless hell has. "God will have mercy on whom he will have mercy" does not mean that He won't eventually have mercy on us all.

To me, endless hell is not a "seeming contradiction between God's righteousness and His love", it is rather <u>an absolute contradiction</u>.

Bob, your paragraph describing your attitude of submission to God perfectly describes the way I would like my attitude towards God to be, but your assertion that He will do whatever is right and loving cannot in my mind include allowing His created beings to suffer endlessly in a hell the like of which Jesus described.

Your comments concerning the Ohio lady also showed me that you lack understanding. This lady did indeed by her acts of murder make it impossible for her infants to be cast into an endless hell. Bob, the issue here is not "long term" or "short term"; the issue is NEVER COMING TO AN END!

Obviously the love of the mother for the infants out-weighed her respect for the commandment of God not to kill. She may have believed that she herself would be put into an endless hell for what she did, but she would think to herself, "At least I have insured the salvation of the infants that I learned to love so deeply in the few short months that I had them in my care", and she would be absolutely right. It is still my point of view that the action of this lady was perfectly rational and a natural outcome of her theology. It is your attempt to discredit the rationality of it that I find illogical.

You also lack understanding concerning the matter of suicide. Bob, I tell you plainly that there is an intensity of suffering which if prolonged for an indefinite length of time make the commandment of God "Thou shalt not kill" totally irrelevant to the person who is contemplating suicide. When the suffering becomes unbearable then the whole motivating force of the person's entire being is directed toward gaining relief. They are not even capable of caring about what God thinks.

I wish I had the power of being able to let people experience what hell is like for just a few seconds. Any person's theology would undergo a drastic change in those few seconds! It's like my former pastor once said, "Five minutes of experience is more convincing than many volumes of theological arguments!" The words of Jesus describing hell are <u>no exaggeration at all</u>.

If I were to actually believe you, that "any hope that is at a lower level than confidence is of the devil," I would be overwhelmed with despair. The hope that God has allowed me to have is the most precious thing in my life. Without it I would either withdraw from reality (go insane), or I would commit suicide in a desperate attempt to find out what the truth really is.

Bob, I don't see that my faith in Christ has weakened one iota, but I do see that my faith in the former concept that I used to try to have of Christ has been shattered beyond repair.

(Note: I was totally unaware of having written this last statement of faith until I read it over. I realize that my endless hell friends will be quick to point out that I really don't have faith in Christ, just faith in an unscriptural figment of my unsanctified imagination. But never-the-less it gave me no small thrill to read what obviously poured forth out of my subconscious. I wasn't even aware that I had any faith at all!)

Bob, your exhorting me to pick up the shield of faith to ward off the fiery darts of Satan that are trying to stop me from believing in an endless hell, is like telling a crippled person to get up and walk, without imparting the power that is needed to cause the crippled person's faith to be rewarded.

Bob, to a psycho-neurotic like myself, your statement "fear is not a fruit of the Spirit," is just about the worst possible thing you could say. A neurotic concludes that God must surely be against him because he is not able to stop being afraid, and this overwhelming conclusion, in turn, is the cause of experiencing more intense fear than ever before. The psycho-neurotic's sickness is essentially the inability to stop being afraid, and in this state all the promises and exhortations of scripture simply backfire and cause him to be worse off than he was before. It would be better just to pray to God for me and say you are not able to understand my problem but that you sympathize, than to exhort me to do what I cannot do.

Bob, the subjective experience of my nervous breakdown is far, far more powerful than all the "objective evidences" that endless hell people use to try to get me to believe their way.

Once again I state my position clearly: To say that God is just and loving and good on the one hand, but then to say He allows us to choose our destiny by a succession of choices that results in our winding up in a state like Jesus describes; and then to say that He never, ever lets them out of that condition, is a total mockery of the word "justice", and makes the idea of fair play in justice a total absurdity. God has got to be able to do better than that. As my father says, "Even I could do better than that!"

I do want to thank you for your concern for me which I know is what motivated your letter.

Sincerely

Roger

Dear Roger:

I have your open letter before me and after reading it, I must feel something like you do, only for a different reason. I am glad you use the word "hope," but I am sorry you do not have that real faith and joy in the Lord that His mercy and lovingkindness warrants.

The "endless hell" idea seems to be a fixation with you. Our God is a loving Heavenly Father. He is described over and over again in the Bible as being abundant in mercy. If anyone will be lost forever, it is because he wants to be lost; that is, he refuses God's mercy.

There are some people who would rather have their own way in hell than submit to God and His kingdom.

I don't think your experience while having a nervous breakdown is a valid description of hell. We really don't know what hell is. We do know it is separation from God, but no one will be separated from God who doesn't want to be.

How God deals with those who have never heard, I don't know. I do know that He will deal with them according to His own holy and loving character.

Having know God for almost fifty years, and having studied His word since my conversion, I am more than ever convinced of the goodness of God. I don't dwell on the fate of those who reject Him. I do know that incorrigibles have to be segregated. One sin spoiled this earth. God is not going to take a chance that sin will break out again in heaven. Just how God will deal with the finally impenitent and those who refuse to submit to Him, I don't know, but I do know His character, which is holy, good, loving, kind and patient, will not be compromised.

Of course, those who refuse to submit will be excluded from heaven. There is a place prepared for the devil and his followers. There is a rival kingdom. Those who choose that, rejecting the kingdom of God, know what they are doing.

God has revealed His love towards us through His Son, who suffered untold agony and made full atonement so that we and all who will repent and believe may be saved. He has proven His love on Calvary's cross, and He revealed it before and afterwards. Our God is a loving Heavenly Father worthy to be honored, loved, trusted and obeyed. I know He will do everything right and everything good. He is longing for you to trust Him, not only to hope but to believe Him. If you do He will reveal Himself to you in a new way.

I don't know what else to say. I have a feeling your mind is made up. I can say this on the authority of God's word: he is love – that He loves you – that He is worthy to be trusted. If you fully commit yourself and all your questions and problems to Him, He will give you peace beyond understanding.

The Bible says, "In nothing be anxious; but by prayer and supplication with thanksgiving let your requests be known unto God. And the peace of God, which passeth all understanding, shall guard your hearts and you thoughts in Christ Jesus." I know this to be true. May you accept it as truth.

May God bless you and help you in every way. We pray for you.

Yours in Christ

"T"


Note: It is a fact that I have a great deal of respect for the writer of this last letter, but what he is saying deeply disturbs me. Jesus' description of hell fits the experience of my nervous breakdown. In that state I was totally preoccupied with my suffering. It would have been impossible for me to function in opposition to God. What the writer of the last letter is in essence saying, is that God is going to grant the rebellious an extra supply of supernatural power that increases their capability so they can both suffer like Jesus describes and function in opposition to God at the same time, and be fixed in that state eternally! This concept of "justice" causes me to respond like Abraham Lincoln did. When an evangelist told him he had to get "saved" or he would be punished with unspeakable torment forever, Lincoln replied, "Sir, your God is my devil!"

The following is my reply to his letter:

Dear "T":

Thank you for your letter that I received today.

I have a deep respect for you because you have God's blessing upon you and God has prospered you and yours abundantly. This is a good thing and I am glad to see it. I can say this sincerely without a sour grapes attitude because if God is like I hope He is, then both your spiritual prosperity and my lack of it is going to work out for His glory.

You say in your letter that you have a feeling that I have made up my mind. Frankly I wish I could, because then I think my suffering would cease.

Your asking me to exercise faith is like asking a crippled person to rise up and walk without imparting the power necessary to cause their faith to be rewarded. It causes me great emotional pain for you to exhort me to do it when I can't.

I don't know what's going on in my life if God is like I hope He is then everything will work out better that I went through this – better than if I hadn't gone through it. I intend to see it through as long as I can tolerate the suffering. I cast myself upon the Lord with all the hope within me.

For the past ten years I have been clearing the ground in my mind of the objective reasons why I should not place my hope in the total-restoration interpretation of scripture, although the subjective experience of my nervous breakdown is a far greater personal convincer than any "objective evidence" or the respect I have for any man, no matter how much they have been blessed by God.

My present emotional stability, such as it is, is entirely dependant on hoping that two facts are totally incompatible and cannot exist at the same time – and these two so-called "facts" are: that God is essentially good, loving and just, and that the sufferings of hell never come to an end.

The hell that Jesus describes is a perfect description of what I went through, and no being would be able to experience it for even a few minutes without changing his mind about his attitude towards God.

To say that God created beings that have the capacity to choose their way into such a state, and God will never allow it to come to an end, is making a mockery out of the definition of justice, let alone love. I am hoping with all the hope within me that the word "goodness" cannot be attached to such an action .

I want to appeal to you on the grounds of your memory of the opposition you had when your group first started, and how you wished that people would not be so closed minded to the ideas that you felt God was revealing to your little starting nucleus.

I realize that you believe God doesn't want you to detour from the emphasis that you have been majoring on since the beginning, yet would you consider the possibility that you may not have yet had a full revelation of God's ultimate purpose.

I am sending you a bundle of books written by men who love holiness and abhor any "gospel" that condones loose living. But what their interpretation of scripture does to the character of God is breathtakingly glorious!

Because my emotional state is fragile, I am asking you to please not tell me any of your negative reactions to this material. Probably the only thing that is keeping me from becoming completely unhinged at this point in my life is my hope that these people are right in their concept of what God is like.

I am not sending this material to anyone else in your group. I know you will appreciate this fact. I recognize you as God's anointed leader and it is right and proper that you should screen any foreign ideas that might unsettle the minds of the members of your flock.

(Editor's note: According to Ray Prinzing the Bible does not teach that hell is separation from God, but hell is of a limited duration will take place "in the presence of the Lamb and His holy angels." Neither does the Bible teach that there will be a rival kingdom eternally functioning in opposition to God. Neither does it teach that God created beings that become "incorrigible."

Whether the reader judges me right or wrong, it is a fact that my own personal feelings or security depend on the hope that the letter write "T" is wrong and Ray Prinzing is right. I personally am not "saved." I do not have the "witness of the Spirit that I am a child of God." All I have is hope that hell for me will come to an end. I cannot put my trust in a god who allows his created beings to suffer endlessly.)

Letter to "T" continued:

If you will permit me a word of observation to the end that it might be constructive criticism; From my vantage point, to the extent that I have been involved with people from your group, I see three kingdoms trying to rule in people's hearts.

One of them, the kingdom of Satan, is the least you have to

be concerned with, because your people are well practiced at repelling his attempted inroads into their hearts.

By far the one they should have the greatest concern about is the kingdom of your group itself that so often is manifested in the words of those who love the group. From my observation it is evident that the kingdom of the group is not always synonymous with the kingdom of God. In the hearts of your people the "group kingdom" must and will sooner or later be destroyed so that only the pure kingdom of God remains. The sooner it is destroyed in each individual heart, the better off that person will be, and it naturally follows that the group as an entity will be better off too.

May God bless you abundantly even as He has in the past, and my sincere hope is that you will continue to prosper in all that you set your heart to do, for I know that your attitude, that is your motive (God's glory) is at the center of everything you do. Pray for me please!

Sincerely,

Roger


Dear Roger:

Thanks for sending us a copy of your letter. When we read it our hearts went out to you. We really appreciated you sharing with us your inner feelings. I think that is about the hardest thing for all of us to do.

My husband and I were talking about your letter. The conclusion we came to is that there is no pat answer to any problem or difficulty for someone to give to another. We are believing that somehow the cry of your heart will find an answer.

We love you very much and it hurts us to see you hurting. I'm not just writing this because it might sound good. We really both love you and are concerned when you aren't happy.

If there is anything we can do to help, please let us know.

We love you Roger.

    "L" & "D"

The couple who wrote this last letter, I consider to be my best endless hell friends. They came to visit me a short time after I received their letter. The husband listened to me empty out my soul for seven hours straight. When I finished he said, "Roger, you are not the person I thought you were."

I asked him if he agreed with what other people have said about me, that he would have to stand at the judgment and tell me, "I tried to tell you so" as he watched me being banished into an endless hell of torment.

His answer was short and seriously somber. He said, "I don't know."

When he said that I broke out into a fear sweat and my old nervous breakdown feelings began to crowd in on top of me.

## I DON'T WANT TO GO TO AN ENDLESS HELL!!!

I will do absolutely anything I can not to go there. I would even violate my conscience if I could be sure it would prevent me from going to an endless hell. And believe me, it would be a violation of my conscience to try to believe in the doctrine of an endless hell. God knows my heart and my attitude, but I have to say in the strongest possible terms that the god of an endless hell is, in my mind, the sum total of everything that is hideously evil and vile. It's like trying to convince me that Satan is really God. There is just simply no way that I can even begin to try to believe it. But I can tell you for sure that if I thought believing in an endless hell would prevent me from going there I would try to believe it in a big hurry! I have experienced a state of being that fits the Biblical description of hell and there is absolutely nothing that I would not do if I thought it would insure me against going back into that state of being without end!

I felt I lost my best endless hell friend during that conversation. And I can't help wondering – if this is what happened with my best friend, then what's going to happen when my other endless hell friends read my manuscript?

The frankness of the contents of this book may cause me to lose some friends. But I am hoping that if they can bear with me through this whole book that I will be able to develop new friendships with the same people on a different level of understanding. If you can still love me in spite of what you are going to learn about me then your friendship will be a precious treasure to me.

Dear Roger:

I don't think you were asking for an answer to the doctrinal question, from me anyway. I don't have one for you. I only hurt for you – I know you are hurting.

I'm glad you have Helen. I admire her – she's a lot of things I'm not.

Thank you for sharing your feelings with me. I don't know how or when your answer will come. Only don't give up hope.

Sorry I can't help with the answer.

Love you guys.

"C"

Note: I have always liked "C" very much and I was grateful for her note of sympathy.

Dear "C":

Thank you for your note.

Somehow it helps to know that people like you know about my problem and care.

"T" still doesn't understand. He says, "I see that you've made up your mind." If I could make up my mind I wouldn't be in this state.

He insists that I exercise faith when all I have is hope. To me it's like asking a crippled person to get up and walk without imparting to them the power to cause their faith to be rewarded. It wouldn't hurt so much if I didn't respect him as much as I do.

I don't know what's going on in my life but I intend to see it through as long as I can tolerate the suffering.

Thanks "C"!

>Roger


Dear Roger:

Shalom!

I would like to respond briefly to your open letter awaiting me when we got home this evening. I was deeply touched by your honesty and deep sense of need. I think you understand already that at no time have I ever thought less of you or condemned you for your views regarding hell. I myself have never been very dogmatic regarding this doctrinal issue, tending to prefer a preoccupation with the positive rather the negative.

I am truly saddened by the torment that you apparently suffer regarding it however. I remember the glimpses I had of your suffering at the time of your nervous breakdown, and though I will likely never be able to appreciate what you went through, I am convinced of the reality of its horror for you. And I have admired the recovery you have made – many people never do recover.

I would like to try to help you, Roger, by sharing several of my personal beliefs concerning the nature of God. I prefer to talk about Him rather than hell, believing the latter comes into focus better as we look at God, its creator.

There are several very basic attributes of God that bear heavily on this, these are that He is love, and He is holy. To me, these and all His other attributes are not, indeed cannot be contradictory.

The Bible reveals to me that because of God's holiness he demands that sin be dealt with, which means that the sinner is called upon to repent or suffer the consequences.

Because of God's love He provided a means of salvation through the indescribable sacrifice of Calvary by which sin was removed or atoned for.

There remains only the application of this atonement through personal acceptance, through believing faith in Christ.

Where this atonement is rejected, man must experience for himself in judgment what Christ already did as our substitute. For I understand the Bible to say that Jesus went to hell for us – His crucifixion was not hell as awful as that was. He in fact went to the place of torment and did indeed suffer its fury.

But His suffering was not eternal was it? It was in the framework of time, and it seems to me reasonable to assume that the unrepentant sinner's suffering will also be in the framework of time.

Now, coming out of God's holiness is His justice. "Will not the God of all the earth do right?" God asked Abraham rhetorically. Of course He will. He must, or deny and contradict His own nature. Therefore the sentence received will be utterly fair. Of that I am convinced. But that sentence is not the same for all. "Some will be beaten with few stripes and others with many," noted Jesus. There are indeed degrees of punishment in hell. And I'm not talking about heat measurement in its flames – more probably duration than intensity.

I also do not think of God as being destructive – He wounds in order to heal. To me the concept of judgment being corrective instead of destructive is much more appealing.

Do not be overwhelmed by the numbers for or against an issue or truth. The majority vote is often the wrong choice. Just as it is a remnant who will be saved, that is won to Christ and serve Him during their earthly lives, so also only a remnant grasp many of the basic truths.

Dwell on the love, mercy, patience, longsuffering and justice of our holy God, and hell is less terrible. Not that we should not shun it, but that it is within the bounds of the Blessed Lord worthy of all our adoration and dedicated service.

I don't plan to get anywhere near it. Which brings me to an important point for you to ponder and maybe write back to me about – namely, your assurance of salvation , its basis etc., or lack of it.

Meanwhile, let me assure you and your family of our love and sincere interest and concern.

PS: Two more thoughts: Even David echoed many doubts and fears – why hide them when God knows anyway.

Salvation is not based on belief in a doctrine, but in THE PERSON. May His Name be praised!

"A"

Note: The writer of the last letter graduated from an endless hell Bible school. I was pleased to learn that even though he is the pastor of a church, he does not believe in endless hell. The following letter is my reply to him.

Dear "A":

Thank you for your letter.

It strengthens my hope to find out that although you don't consider the endless hell issue to be of major importance as I do, yet you still don't think that it is indeed endless.

To me it is the only really important issue in this life, because from my point of view, it is the deciding factor in judging whether or not God is essentially good. If it can be proven objectively, and the majority say it can, that hell is without end, then I think it best to hope that there is a stronger God that has not yet been revealed that can overthrow the rulership of this one.

I am hoping that God's character is such that He allows all evil for a good purpose, and that there is nothing at all that

He allows to happen that He hasn't already figured out He is going to make it better that it happened than had it not happened for everyone concerned.

It is totally impossible for me to believe two so-called facts at the same time: that God is essentially good, and that hell is without end.

I very much appreciated your words of comfort and your attitude of trying to understand my problem. I would need an ample supply of this attitude to hold me steady if Helen should die, and I am, and have been in such a state for the past ten years, that if an endless hell person tried to comfort me I would be sorely tempted to kill them on the spot.

You once suggested that I might seek help from a certain evangelical counselor. I tell you plainly that no endless hell person would be able to minister to me effectively, no matter how kind and understanding they might be.

I envy your ability to be preoccupied with the positive rather than the negative.

I am very much aware of the attributes of God that you want me to draw my attention to, but they all become a mockery and the ultimate in absurdity if the sufferings that Jesus describes as hell, never comes to an end.

I appreciate the simple gospel message that you wrote to me. Certainly this is the sole basis of my hope if indeed hell is not endless, and therefore the God of the Bible is good.

Your most helpful exhortation was the one that said not to be overwhelmed by the numbers who are for an endless hell. The first letter that I sent to you I also sent to fourteen key people, and I am hoping that the result will be that I will be able to break free from the bondage of their opinion.

I don't believe that my own personal assurance of salvation, or lack of it is a relevant issue at this time. I think that everyone will experience hell to the extent that they have not been conformed to the image of Christ in this life. But I look on hell as a friend, not an enemy. I think that hell is the very best that the loving heart of God can do for those who do not allow themselves to be completely conformed to His image. It takes on an entirely different character when looked at that way.

Thanks again for your letter.

     Roger

---

Dear Roger:

Your letter came a few minutes ago and it has put me before our loving and lovely Lord in prayer for you, His dear child.

This is the first time I've ever heard that you had a nervous breakdown.

The older I grow the more I understand how great is God's love. He takes into account millions of circumstances in the lives of struggling humanity – what influences bore in upon them even in their mother's womb. And He cares – what greater proof of this do we need as we think of His having given us His best – even Jesus?

I do not think of hell, endless or otherwise. My vision is filled with Him who is altogether lovely and my business is to lift Him up by my life and my words.

If I had my life to live over again, I would no permit myself to be negative. Thank God it is even now not too late. I refuse to let Satan rob me of the power to appropriate all that Jesus is and wants to be, for me, in me and through me.

I pray that He will give you His peace. He is going to bring you out into the sunlight of His glorious Person.

I love you Roger.

     Lillian


Dear Aunt Lillian:

Thank you for your letter.

I envy your ability not to think about hell.

Because of what I have gone through, my point of view as to whether Jesus is "altogether lovely" or not has become dependant on whether or not the hell that Jesus describes ever comes to an end. I know this sounds blasphemous to evangelicals, never-the-less it's absolutely true.

The biggest hurt that I experience is the well meaning admonition to exercise faith, especially when I am well acquainted with the scriptures they quote to back it up. It's like telling a crippled person to rise up and walk without imparting the power that causes their faith to be rewarded.

Most people can't understand what it is like not to be able to exercise simple faith in the goodness of God.

I don't know what's going on in my life but if God is like I hope He is, then He has a good purpose for my last ten years of suffering. I wish I had <u>faith</u> like you, but since I don't, I throw myself on God's mercy with all the <u>hope</u> within me.

I envy your ability to think positively rather than negatively, but at the same time I am saddened because I know that you cannot truly sympathize with me since my experience is foreign to you.

Love

    Roger

Dear Roger:

A strange thing happened this morning.

I sat here and read your letter, then immediately I picked up my copy of the Pulpit Digest and read the sermon by Ernest Thompson, HE DESCENDED INTO HELL.

Was this a coincidence?

I pray that it may be of help to you.

I have been living in hell for three months but I <u>know</u> that Jesus loves me and isn't going to let go of me.

We will be praying for you.

Your friend in Christ

   Alf

PS: Thanks for sending me your letter.


Dear Pastor Alf:

Thank you for your letter and the article. I am hoping that what the article says is true – that the sufferings of hell are not endless.

I am greatly relieved to find out that you do not believe the suffering of hell are without end. It would have been a crushing blow to find out that you were an endless hell person.

Your sermons and your personality have been an immense encouragement to me over the past two years and they have been a major factor in keeping me hoping in a concept of a good God, so you can understand how painful it would have been to find out that you believed that the sufferings of hell never come to an end.

If I could only shake the influence of the majority who say that only a few will be saved, but most will be tormented endlessly in the kind of hell that Jesus describes. Most "Christians" say that anyone who dares to think differently is rebelling against the plain word of God. My strong hope is that I will soon be able to rid myself of the extraordinary power that this majority has over me.

I wish I had faith in your concept of God, but I want you to know that I pray with all the hope within me that God will minister to you in your own personal hell, for your benefit and His glory. I am hoping that He is so good that He has a wonderful, magnificent purpose for allowing all these "hells" we experience.

Sincerely

Roger

Dear Brother Roger:

Just this morning our mutual friend and brother in Christ brought your letter over to share with us. In reading it I was filled with compassion, and you have been on my heart and in my prayers. My heart cries out to you and you dear wife and children, who I know must be suffering with you in your inability to accept by faith what our dear Lord and Savior is obviously quickening to you.

I know in my Spirit – God's Spirit within me – that you already believe in your spirit, and that you must not fight it or try so hard yourself – just accept your situation, and wait on the Lord to work it out in your heart. Bring your unbelief to the cross and try to leave it there. Let it be crucified with Christ once and for all, as you surrender it the best you can.

I know that He is faithful by the way that He has worked in my life, and what He has done for me, He will also do for you – He loves us all so much.

I was a real dyed-in-the-wool ......., but because the Lord knew my hungry heart yearned for more of Him He led me into the baptism with the Holy Spirit. Then through the ministry of Ed Gregory and Ray Prinzing, I began to see the greatness of our God and to believe in the restitution of all things. I must admit that God made it easy for me to accept and I thank and praise Him for that.

But I was left out of all fellowship with former friends and had accusations made against me and was asked to quit teaching Sunday School.

That's when the Lord really began to deal with me – my life became one crisis after another, which drew me closer and closer to Him as there was no one else that could help.

In His sovereign way He led me through a series of events that brought me here to work with Ed & Liz Gregory in Mississippi from my home in Libby, Montana. It wasn't easy to make the move in the face of all the opposition of my family and friends, but the Lord kept me steadfast and I thank and praise Him that He has brought me here, where I am learning to love Him more and see His hand in everything that happens to us. I am firmly convinced that nothing happens outside the will of God and that He is going to work everything out in our lives for our good and for His glory.

We can't understand His ways nor know His thoughts – except to know that He loves us and sooner or later because He loves you He is going to bring peace to your troubled heart and still all of your fears as you flow into His love and know beyond the shadow of a doubt that He is a good God and could never permit even the smallest of His creatures to suffer endlessly!!

We are praying for you and sending kind and loving thoughts which we know will be helpful to you.

God bless all of you richly in His love.

"I"

PS: One other thought Hannah Hurnard brought to mind – that God is suffering through this with you. He is in all of your fears and doubts. Isn't that wonderful to know?

Dear "I":

Thank you for your kind letter.

Thank you especially for sharing my suffering before the Lord in prayer. If He is like I hope He is then He certainly is suffering through his with me.

I do cast myself on Him. I long to do it in faith, but in the mean time I do it with all the hope within me. Faith will come in due time, I hope! Maybe even joy will be mine in this lifetime?!

It is good to hear from yet another person who has faith in such a glorious concept of God.

One thing you said was amusing to us in a sad sort of way because of its irony. The words, "bring your unbelief to the cross and let it be crucified with Christ once and for all" are also being used by my endless hell friends, only the unbelief they are referring to is my inability to love and trust a God who allows His created beings to suffer endlessly.

If God is like I hope He is then He is sovereignly controlling my lack of faith and joy for a certain good reason that is presently not known to me.

Most people cannot even begin to imagine the suffering that I have experienced during the past ten years. It's going to be awfully disappointing if it doesn't turn out that there was a good purpose for it all.

Right now, things are pretty grim from my point of view but my hope is strengthened more and more when I learn of others who also find it impossible to love and trust a god who allows his created beings to suffer endlessly.

Thank you so much for taking the time to write. I can't tell you just how much this letter means to me.

Sincerely

    Roger

Dear Brother Jones:

We have received your long letter and it sounds very much like a cry for help. We want to assure you that God is like you hope He is.

Rather than try to write a long letter we are mailing you a few copies of our publication (THE PAGE) that you may not have as well as a few smaller booklets on the subject, and are asking you to read them slowly, carefully and prayerfully while you trust the Lord to make these truths real to your heart. When this happens it will banish your fears about an endless hell and you will love God for His great and marvelous plan for His creation.

Let God speak by His Spirit; then close your ears to all other voices and rest in the knowledge of the truth that has been revealed to you.

In my opinion you can do yourself nothing but great harm by continually trying to settle all the arguments that people present.

Read the articles I have sent to you and let God speak to you personally. Never mind what other people believe.

A person does not have to be 100% right to be accepted by God.

Sincerely,

George Hawtin


Dear Pastor Hawtin:

Thank you for your good letter. I am looking forward to reading the material you are sending.

I am hoping that with the help of total-restorationist people like yourself that I will be able to free myself from the influence of my endless hell friends. It has taken me ten years to solve the various problems that endless hell people have presented me with in connection with the interpretation of scripture.

Thank you again for your encouragement. Sincerely –

Roger

Note: The freedom that I am seeking, that I referred to in the last letter, is not simply just the ability to ignore the arguments with an alternative point of view based on objective evidence. My conscience cannot accept any other grounds of acceptance of the total-restorationist interpretation of scripture.

Even more important than being intellectually convinced is my need for a personal revelation from God that He will not allow any of His created beings to suffer endlessly. I think that all the objective evidence in the world is useless unless the Holy Spirit of God personally makes it real to my heart.


Dear Roger:

Blessings to you in the joy of the Lord and His victory!

We received the open letter which you prepared and sent out, and we'll take this moment to assure you that you are in His hands, and out of all this deep questioning and struggling to embrace the truth and come into a freedom in the love of God, there is victory to be found.

He will bring you into that joy and victory in due time.

As much as lieth within you, release yourself into His love. Love never faileth, and since God is love, He has a purpose to be fulfilled which leads into ultimate victory.

"Eternal torment" teachers simply have not been quickened by the Spirit to see the whole scope of God's love and grace, and any time we limit God we limit also the redemptive work of God in us.

I know that we cannot live on a borrowed revelation, but we can cast ourselves upon the Lord for His quickening, and He does not cast us aside.

It has been a deep valley, but you will come through. And when you see the truth of His triumph at Calvary, it will be yours too.

Glad to send along the tapes and books you requested.

We trust you understand, but we feel led not to send them to "T". He has met us personally, and taken somewhat of a stand against the things we teach, and therefore we do not feel that he would be open to receive from us. But the Lord can cause another to minister to him of these truths if it is his time to receive.

Concerning Bullinger, what does it prove that he believed in total restoration and later changed his mind. What about some of the men who first taught the rapture theory, and then before their death repudiated the whole idea because they said God showed them it was false. Nobody ever mentions that when they teach the said doctrine of the "rapture", which we also personally believe is false.

These arguments which people have presented to you are based on faulty man's reasonings, not the revelation of the Spirit for truth. We do not mean to be harsh in our speaking on them – but simply they do not qualify as good arguments.

Praise God, He will lead you into more of Himself.

Love in Christ

    Ray Prinzing

Note: It is impossible for me to communicate on paper the immeasurable worth to my own soul of the fortnightly publication (GOSPEL ECHOES) and the cassette sermons (also fortnightly) by Ray Prinzing.

Every passage of scripture takes on a brand new dimension. The character of God is magnified beyond anything I've ever heard before. I find myself saying over and over, "Now that's more like God" and a temporary spurt of joy floods my soul. Sometimes I burst out laughing and my hands and fingers tingle with the thrill of strengthened hope that maybe God really is like that after all.

Then sometimes my laughter turns into a crying spell as I pour out to my wife the frustration I feel that overwhelms me when I think of the insistence of my endless hell friends that God really isn't like that – that it's just wishful unsanctified thinking that hasn't been taken to the cross – that it's in direct opposition to the word of God and I have no business questioning God's ways, since they are far above ours and past finding out.

Ray Prinzing is a man who loves holiness and hates sin. He is a man who wants only what God wants. His expositions are absolutely the most thrilling words that I have ever heard and my whole insides ache and cry out, "Please Jesus – please turn out to really be like that!"

The following is my reply to his letter.

Dear Pastor Prinzing:

Thank you for your encouraging letter. It is especially helpful to me because I am getting some negative feedback from my endless hell friends.

Over the past ten years I have gradually been able to find intellectually satisfying answers to the arguments of the endless hell people.

Although I have a measure of hope subjectively, I want to completely clear the ground of obstacles to faith based on an objective confidence in the total-restoration interpretation of scripture.

More than anything else I need the personal revelation that you speak of. I hope God will soon grant me this so I can stop living on a borrowed revelation.

Since I am not able to cast myself upon the Lord in <u>faith</u> at this present time, I do so with all the <u>hope</u> within me.

Thanks again for your glorious expositions on the character of God.

Sincerely,

Roger

Did you ever get the feeling that maybe everyone else in the world was crazy except you!?

Let me ask you – why is Satan endowed with the fantastic degree of emotional stability that he enjoys? If God would allow him to be in the state that I was in ten years ago even for a short time, he would completely reverse his attitude of rebellion against God. If you question this then I would have to conclude that either you are mentally deficient or that you are unable to comprehend the hideousness of the stark raving terror that I experienced during 1966-68! Jesus' description of hell quite adequately describes what I went through.

Let me ask you again! Why does Satan enjoy the remark-able degree of emotional stability needed to lead a rebellion against God?

Let me tell you what I hope. I hope it's because God is such a great God that He has a fantastically wonderful plan for every being He has created, including Satan. I hope the kind of God that I serve controls the interplay of good and evil, and that in every individual He allows their limited free will to succeed in the direction of evil only as far as it will be useful in fashioning that individual to fit into the plan that He has beforehand decided He wants them to fit into.

This has just got to be true for with just the "flick of a switch" He could plunge Satan into the experience that I was in and convince him once and for all that it simply is just not worthwhile to take a stand of rebellion against God!

What a terrible concept of God the endless hell people have! – That God decided to create beings knowing that the vast majority of them would make a succession of choices what would destine them to function as a separate kingdom against God, and at the same time that He is granting them the strength to function against Himself, He is also allowing them to experience the incredible degree of torment that Jesus describes as hell. And to top it off, they insist that this condition will never, never come to an end. And then they ask us to attach the attributes of love that never fails, mercy that endures aioniously, and justice that is supposed to be the fairest justice in the universe to this concept of how God is going to punish the rebellious.

I honestly don't know how people can stop from going insane when they believe their own personal Savior is like this!

A psychiatrist who was trying to help me during my breakdown asked me if I was an evangelical. He said it's a well known fact among their profession that the majority of neurotic breakdowns are among evangelicals. I know that my evangelical friends would hasten to defend themselves on the grounds that Satan bothers them more than he does other people. But I suspect that the breakdowns occur because of the concept of God they adhere to.

I think that each person is conformed into the image of their concept of God. If they believe in a God who gives up on people then they will also give up on people. If they believe in a God who created a being called Satan who will be successful in deceiving the majority of the people, which will result in their being sealed into a state of never ending suffering, then this concept will manifest itself in their attitudes and their conduct toward others, and they will be able to justify themselves by believing that God is going to do a lot worse than that.

Even from personal experience I am better able to understand the attitudes manifested by the words of my evangelical friends as I recall incident and incident, from all the way back to my childhood, through my years at Bible school, and my seven years as a missionary – to the present time.

My evangelical friends say that I'm being lulled to sleep by a false hope. They say my faith is not in God but rather in a false concept of God based on wishful thinking, and that my basic attitude is sinful and will result in disaster for me, and if I don't repent soon may well result in the eternal damnation of my immortal soul.

They also exhort me to "think of how terrible it will be if my concept of God does not turn out to be true."

I want to declare that the God that I hope in is even in charge of my deceptions and I commit all my hopes to Him, hoping that He will not allow me to stay in a deceived condition any longer than it takes for Him to accomplish the purpose for which He allowed me to be deceived in the first place. This is the kind of God that I want to serve!

I abhor evil and I love righteousness. I declare myself to be on God's side – not Satan's. I want what God wants – and if there is an area where I am deceiving myself even about this commitment, then I am hoping that God is so great that He will take care of this problem as well in due time.

The time has come for me to stop messing around and to take decisive action. I want to declare my hopes strong and clear and if you still condemn me and in the time of major crises I find myself unable to cope with the suffering, I may have to make my appeal to a higher court with a bullet to my head. I can hear you immediately respond that this attitude is not of God. That, my friend will remain to be seen. You have better walk inside my skin for awhile before you dare to make that judgment.

All I know is that the concept of God that I have adhered to in hope during the past ten years, to me, in the words of my father, "is more like God". It is the concept that has restored me to my comparatively strong position of emotional health and stability. It is the concept that has drawn out from me feelings of love, worship, joy and adoration instead of cringing apprehension.

As I said before, if I am wrong about anything that I am hoping in right now, I am hoping that God is of such character that He will correct it in due time.

It is my conclusion based on observation that the evangelical kingdom is not synonymous with the kingdom of God. The fact is that the kingdom of Roger Tutt and the evangelical kingdom, and all other kingdoms whether they be personal or organizational, must ultimately be destroyed until only the pure kingdom of God remains.

It is my observation, based on intimate acquaintance, that the evangelical kingdom is tyrannical. Love flows freely in that kingdom as long as one conforms to the system, but when one steps out of line with the system then all the characteristics of their concept of God are brought to bear on the "rebellious" individual.

The god of the evangelical, the one that they serve, is simply not able to hold them fast in spite of their falling into various deceptions.

The reason they defend their position so fiercely, and believe me they do!, is because they believe their destiny is at stake. What a difference it would make if they could find their security in a sovereign Lord Jesus Christ Who holds the eternal destiny of every single being in His own hands of never failing love, and mercy that lasts aioniously (that is as long as it's necessary for anyone to need mercy), and grace beyond the limitation of the power of man's free will!

I ask you the reader, is this not a thrilling concept of God? Is this not the way you really wished He was if it weren't for the fact that you have been taught that you musn't believe that way because the Bible does not reveal Him as being that way?

Instead of simply allowing for another point of view, the subjects of the evangelical kingdom are so convinced they have God's word on almost everything that anyone who disagrees with them is said to be under the control of an evil spirit of deception, or rebellion, or independence, or the spirit of an evil Bible character who won the hearts of the people for his own selfish purposes.

I am apprehensively curious about which spirits they will decide I have. For ten years I have been afraid of the system I came out of. The system fosters fear, and if you don't line up the weapon of fear is used with skill and if it doesn't work on you then at least they have found it to be reasonably effective in preventing others from lining up with the "rebellious one."

Each person is pigeon holed according to the standard set up by the local group.

I want to declare right now that I renounce the concept of God that is held by the evangelical people. And even though I don't have assurance of salvation or the witness of the Spirit that I am a child of God, I embrace, with all the hope within me the concept of God Who is able to hold me secure regardless of any error I might get entangled in.

I hope my God is so great that He will only allow me to stay in my deception until He has accomplished the purpose for which He allowed me to be deceived in the first place. I feel sorry for people who are not able to hope in a God such as this.

Members of any established system, evangelical or otherwise, are unable to allow themselves to even consider another point of view simply because too much is at stake in regards to the reputation and ministry of their system and their own personal security as well.

Within the 200-plus sections of the evangelical kingdom the doctrine of endless hell is wielded as a mighty weapon of fear to keep its subjects of the kingdom in line. It is my observation that it is primarily fear, not love, that motivates nearly all of their actions in connection with their missionary zeal and their interpretation of the Bible which they call the word of God.

Each member gets his feeling of security from defending the "rightness" of their own particular group, and it is my experience that extra-ordinary un-Christ-like attitudes are manifested whenever they system is seriously challenged, and invariably the old faithful weapon of the doctrine of endless hell is brought into use, usually in such a subtle manner that it is hardly recognizable to the conscious mind. They use phrases like, "I'm telling you this because I'm only interested in your eternal welfare."

How I wish people could get their outlook broadened and begin hoping in a God who is bigger than all this nonsense! What a change it would make in their definition of justice, love, mercy and grace!

This use of the weapon of fear to pull a "wayward" subject of the evangelical kingdom back into line nearly always works, for it is an awesome force to contend with when a cell within the evangelical kingdom decides that you have one or more evil spirits connected with you.

What a world of difference there is in the attitude of the total-restoration people who believe that God has all deception under control and will not allow it to be successful any further than He has plans to use the temporary time of deception to accomplish what He wants to accomplish in the heart of the individual!

My hope is that God says, "Alright, if you by the free will that I have given you decide to strike out in a direction of your own then I will let you; but I will only allow you to be successful to the point that what you will learn will ultimately make you more useful in my kingdom."

What a magnificent concept of God this is! And what a frightening, binding concept is the one held by the 200-plus sections within the evangelical kingdom.

The possibility of new light coming into an established kingdom is very small, because all of the safeguards that are operating to keep out heresy are also preventing the recognition of new truths. However, the established kingdoms, including evangelicalism, will only function as long as God has a purpose in allowing them to do so. Babylon, all institutionalized Christianity including evangelicalism, "is a golden cup in the hands of the Lord," but when God is finished with Babylon its systems will be destroyed, although all people both without and within its systems will be saved.

Their psychological safeguards, based on the assertions that "God said it" make the evangelical systems every bit as tyrannical as any other religious system. These safeguards are reinforced with stories of how God struck down by unusual accident, or caused to go insane anyone who stepped out of line.

More than several times I have listened with a heavy heart to members of the system who spoke with despising words of condemnation whenever names were raised of anyone who found the courage to challenge the system.

On the basis of these past experiences I cannot help but experience apprehension about my evangelical friends' attitude towards myself. I have actually had the phraseology used on me, "If you don't line up I will turn the whole fellowship against you."

To be quite honest about it I would consider it an honor to be struck down by God so I could get away from this mess down here and place myself in the hands of a God Who, I hope, is a good deal more tolerant than the people I know.

Another fear safeguard that is often misused by the evangelicals is the II Tim. 4 passage of scripture that speaks of those with itching ears who seek out preachers that will please them. By wielding this awesome weapon of "God's word" to their own advantage, the 200-pluw sections of the evangelical kingdom are almost certain to keep their followers in line.

Another of the several dangers in the establishment of an organizational kingdom is that too much confidence is placed in methods of problem analysis and solution techniques for the purpose of "trying the spirits to see if they be of God" and establishing other causes for problems. These things may not be wrong in themselves, but when so much confidence is put in the technique it is my observation that when the technique apparently fails, it's the person seeking help that is condemned instead of the technique.

I have been told more than once that the safest choice was to stick with the endless hell belief because the majority down through the centuries believed it. Even if the majority did believe it, one would on the basis of the same logic have to reject the crises of entire sanctification. I choose this doctrine for it is mostly people from this theological persuasion that have used this argument on me.

In the Christian world where nearly everyone is familiar with the teachings of Christianity, the doctrine of eternal hell is probably the primary cause for the number of agnostics and infidels there are. Evangelicals think its because they love sin and don't want to be bothered with a God who might restrict their independent style of life, but the real reason is probably the incompatability between the doctrine of endless hell on the one hand and the assertions of the justice and love and God on the other.

People who believe in total-restoration, approach witnessing with the highest level of confidence for they believe that every effort they put forth will be the link in a chain of events that leads that soul away from independent self government to participatory function within the kingdom of God. However they do not believe that the salvation of others is <u>dependent</u> on their effort.

The value and power of free will has been highly overestimated. It is my hope that God will interfere with man's free will for his own good.

When I asked my father, who has recently become a total-restorationist why God allowed this endless hell theology to prosper so, this was his answer: "When God told Moses to step aside while He destroyed Israel from the face of the earth, Moses could have said, 'Who am I to question God?', instead of interceding for the people. And on the same basis, God is looking for those whose concept of His age-abiding mercy and never failing love causes them to cry out, 'For your name's sake' Lord, let not one single soul remain outside the changing power of the redemption of Jesus Christ!"

The following is my statement of HOPE, based on the total-restoration interpretation of scripture. These hopes were instrumental in causing my recovery from my nervous breakdown. They are what I, Roger Tutt, have hoped in from 1966-76. This set of hopes have ministered life to me and continue to do so. This is why I cling to them even in the face of strong opposition.

I, Roger Tutt, HOPE –

That God will erase all the consequences of sin from existence and bring all created beings who continue to exist, into a right relationship with Himself.

That after we have thought the very best thoughts about God, we can be sure He is even better than that.

That many negative things happen to everyone which is beyond their control, but that the character of God is such that He will not just make it up to us, but He will see to it that it was better that the negative thing happened than had it not happened, and that this includes people who do not claim to be "saved" in the evangelical sense. Everyone has some wrong ideas about what God is like. The Bible should be interpreted in a way that glorifies God's character.

That to the degree that a person responds in a positive way to the righteousness of Jesus Christ, (and most people are responding to a degree whether they know His name of not), to that degree they are "born again". We are born again only to the extent that we are conformed to the moral character of Jesus. Everyone is in the fetus stage of spiritual birth.

That we are born spiritually dead and a spiritual conception takes place when we make the first intellectual choice in favor of righteousness, at which time a fetus stage is entered into which is not completed during an earthly lifetime.

That to the degree a person has repented and sought forgiveness for sins committed, to that degree he can be said to be saved from the just punishment deserved for those sins; and to the degree that person has not repented or sought forgiveness, to that degree he will suffer the disciplines of hell.

That heaven and hell are together and can be visualized as a sphere, the center of which is the throne of God. The farther the distance from the center the more like hell it becomes. As water seeks its own level so does the moral character of each individual seek its own closeness to the center. For those, especially children, who fear separation from their loved ones, we can be sure that we will be with them as much as we need to be.

That during the ages to come those who are closer to the center will be busy with the job of bringing those who are further away from the center into greater conformity to Christ. The result will not be that more individuals will move closer to the center necessarily, although they will increasingly feel more at home nearer the center, but rather the quality of life at the center will expand outwards till at the end of the ages to come, at the beginning of eternity, the entire expanse of creation will be free from the effects of sin and every individual will be conformed to the image of Christ. Hell will cease to exist when it has served its purpose of convincing that selfish rebellion is not worthwhile.

That only serving others under the direction of Christ is lastingly worthwhile. Jesus took a towel and washed the disciples' feet as an example of how the greatest person should conduct himself. He said, "He that would be greatest among you must be the servant of all."

That the rewards of heaven are related to increased ability to be useful, and the characteristic of hell is that in the areas that an individual has not yielded to the control of Christ, they become useless. Total hell would be to discover that one is totally useless to everyone including themselves, which would be the result of a total rejection of Christ in every area of their life.

That most people are responding at least a little to the influence of the Holy Spirit towards the righteousness of Christ whether or not they know His name. Farthest out from the center the total Christ rejecters, a comparatively small number, will have to suffer a just retribution for the suffering their sins have caused.

They will be outside the administering portion of the kingdom of God, totally useless to everyone including themselves, with a capacity only to suffer the just consequences. Only after they suffer a just penalty will they be in a condition to be ministered to by those closer to the center. If a person is responding to Christ even a little, God will nurture that response by having them dwell in a part of heaven with persons of like response where those closer to the center will minister to them. God will not snuff out that response by putting them with total Christ rejecters.

By manifesting love and righteousness nearly everyone is responding to the influence of the Holy Spirit. Missionary work is important, not in the evangelical sense – to get people "saved," but rather to introduce people to the One who is causing them to love righteousness. People don't "get saved"; salvation is a process in which <u>everyone</u> is involved. There are more than a dozen books in print that were written to show that hell will not be eternal.

That the words of Jesus reasonably interpreted are authoritative and infallible – the words of God. However some of the words of Jesus are difficult if not impossible to understand and they make on e wonder if He was quoted correctly.

That the actual words of God in the old testament are probably just that – the actual words of God, and the prophecies contained in the old and new testaments may also be of God – time will tell. Although the rest of the Bible contains much good insight on the character of God and human behavior, it is not necessarily the word of God as such. Although much of it is obviously inspired by God because it compliments the words of Jesus, it should be regarded as on a par with the inspired preaching, praying and praising of the people who love God today.

Note: Because sex is such a powerful factor in most of our lives I would like to record here a statement of what I consider to be a healthy attitude towards it. I differ from the evangelicals in that I do not believe that masturbation is a sin.

Here is what I believe: That a person who desires to obey the words of Jesus will not engage in premarital sex. That the intentional stimulation between a man and a woman should occur only between couples who have committed themselves to each other for life. That marriage is difficult at best and sex is meant to be one of the main ingredients that holds a marriage together. That petting is intentional stimulation and therefore is fornication unless the couple are committed to each other for life. That God's judgment of Sodom shows what He thinks about homosexuality and lesbianism. That masturbation is not sinful.

During the last ten years my social life has gradually improved. I now meet and love people because they are people, not on the basis of whether or not they are "saved" or are going to ultimately be a total Christ rejector (and I was taught that most are).

Life is becoming more fun and more worth living, not in the sense of being free to sin, but in the sense of being able to like people just because they are people who will in God's timing find assurance of forgiveness for their sins and be conformed to His image, maybe even with my help!

I rejected evangelicalism because it almost quite literally destroyed me via suicide. I cannot function with evangelicals on a social level without suffering a high degree of emotional pain. Their very existence is a threat to my feelings of security, and the fact that they are kind loving people most of the time is making it extra hard to break free from their influence.

After reading my statement of hope I can envisage some of my evangelical friends, at least in spirit if not literally screaming heresy. I probably already know all the reasonings and arguments that they will want to use to "straighten me out" in my doctrine. I urge them to commit their concern to God even as I have committed my hopes to God, for I rather doubt they could tell me anything that I have not already considered.

During the time that I have been compiling this material I have begun to be aware that the kingdom of man's opinions is beginning to lose a subject. For the first time in my life I am beginning to be truly free. I realize my evangelical friends will say I have a spirit of independence, but this doesn't bother me as much as it used to. I know that God knows what's in my heart and that's good enough for me.

Some will say, "Roger, you are not the person I thought you were", and in a sense I'm glad they say this. For thirty years I pretended to be different than I really was and it's a great relief to know that people are at last finding out what the real me is really like. I may have to make a new set of friends for I know that some will consider it their scriptural duty to separate themselves from me. If some of my past evangelical friends remain my friends I will know the grace of God is working in them more than I thought it might be.

Some have just plainly said, "You have set yourself up in direct opposition to God's word thus condemning yourself by your own words and you will receive a just penalty for it in due time".

I'm not afraid of a just penalty, for it's my hope that all judgment is remedial, therefore I willingly commit myself and all my hopes into God's hands. I am becoming more and more convinced that He doeth all things well.

As I have been working on this project I have been feeling, seeping into all the inmost parts of my soul and spirit, an inner strength that wasn't there before. I know that evangelicals will say it's the strength of Satan, but I prefer to give the glory to God. So be it!

If any of my evangelical friends read my statement of hope, I think I already know the things they would like to say to me. During the first thirty years of my life I became intimately acquainted with their thinking.

Evangelicals may assert that the strength I have received from my hopes over the past ten years is Satanic strength. They may assert that the peace I enjoy each time I think about my hopes is false peace, based on teachings that are in direct opposition to God's word. Never the less what I have is real to me and I am very grateful to God for it.

I don't pretend to be anywhere near the caliber of Job, but I do identify with him somewhat. Some people downgrade Job's friends but I think he had magnificent friends. Who in this world has a friend who would come and be with them and say absolutely nothing for seven days? Most of the friends I have arrived at a solution for me as soon as they learned about my problems. Just because Job's friends came to the wrong conclusion doesn't mean that their attitude wasn't right.

After seven days of concentrated meditation, they felt the safest approach was to declare a solution that to their minds most glorified God even though it mean condemning Job. Their conclusion was wrong but their attitude was right, and this is the way I feel about my evangelical friends.

When all their words of condemning Job came to an end Job prayed for his friends, and God restored the fortunes of Job when he prayed for his friends!

So I say to you my evangelical friend, I am starting as of right now to respond to you in an attitude of prayer to God with the hope that God will restore to me the fortune of a sound mind and stable emotions.

If any of the things you have read are a product of the king-dom of Roger Tutt, I hope that God is of such character that He will firmly but gently take care of it in due time.

A positive change has been taking place deep within me during the hours that I have been working on this project, and I like it; MAN DO I LIKE IT! I sense an inner strength that makes any serious consideration of suicide very far away.

I feel like I have been on a long journey across a very wide desert and I have just now reached the other side and have started to walk on the grassy plain.

Because my hopes are different from your beliefs, you prob-ably can see all sorts of bogs and miry pits that I might fall into, but as for me, through the hope that God has allowed me to have, I look to my Good Shepherd, my Lord Jesus Christ who has complete charge of my journey over the grassy plain. So be it!

This is the end of the matter for now.

May God bless you all real good, even as I can sense He is doing to me.

## CHANGED

Changed, according to the power wherewith he shall sub-due
The host of evil forces rebellion did accrue
Until by grace in triumph He maketh all things new
To bring into subjection the ego of each man

To purge his floor completely, His fan is in His hand
Till all shall bow before Him, all of creation's clan

Changed, according to the purpose of Him who works His
will
In the heart of everyone who waits before Him still
That He might be the fullness which doth their being fill
To bring a sure conclusion to all He hath begun
Conforming to the image, the image of His Son
Till all shall be united, till all in Him are one

Changed, according to His mercy that nought shall yet re-
main
Within corruption's bondage and evil's dark domain
But all shall be delivered, a full redemption gained
To know that glorious freedom where sin and self must
cease
Rejoicing in His glory, the joy of full release
When all if changed forever to know His perfect peace
By Ray Prinzing

If I asked you to read this manuscript it's because I would
like you to be my friend. If you do not think you can be my
friend after you finish reading it, I will understand.

# THE GRASSY PLAIN

The first 37 pages of this book dealt with the first thirty years of my life. It describes my DESERT JOURNEY through evangelicalism and the beginning of my gradual escape from evangelical tyranny. This next portion, THE GRASSY PLAIN describes the continuation of that escape.

Evangelicals are nice, kind, considerate and compassionate people most of the time, and this has made it extra difficult to break away from their influence. The exception to their niceness manifests itself when they defend what they "know" to be the "truth."

God has allowed me to experience the full brunt of their "righteous indignation" and many of these experiences are described in the following pages.

It is taking a long time to sort out what is real and what is phoney in my life, but if God is like I hope He is the process will be completed according to His timing.

I can function comfortably with evangelicals on a business level, that is I can work side by side with them. But I suffer a high degree of emotional pain when I attempt to function with them on a social (fellowship) level. The following pages will help to explain why.

The most precious thing in my life is the HOPE that God has allowed me to have. It gives me reason to want to go on living. The following pages will also help to explain why I have HOPE.

Evangelicals cannot accept that I am believing they way God wants me to believe and am acting the way God wants me to act for this period of time in my life. Consequently I cannot accept their lack of acceptance.

I am going through a process of rejecting much of the evangelical's interpretation of, and attitude towards the Bible and the result has been the nearest thing to being "born again" that I have experienced.

It is my hope that God has allowed the evangelicals to be bound in their error for a good reason. However my hope is not strong enough to enable me to fee comfortable in their presence on a social level.

Evangelicals claim the "KNOW" – they don't just hope – They "KNOW." And even if they concede that they don't know everything for sure they will still insist that they "KNOW" what they have to know for sure and what they don't have to know for sure.

The suffering that I have experienced during the last ten years is beyond most people's imagination. I am asking you to perhaps do a little suffering with me during the following pages, for one of the basic characteristics of a friend is that they are willing to share what is going on inside the true self. They don't just share the more refined aspects of social contact.

A good friend of Madame Guyon, Francois Fenelon, Archbishop of Cambria once said, "The right to be wrong in matters of religious belief must be accorded. Otherwise we produce hypocrites instead of persons with enlightened belief that is fully their own. It the truth be mighty and God all-powerful, we need not fear that disaster will follow freedom of thought."

Evangelicals teach a combination of things that I have just not been able to cope with emotionally. On the one hand they teach that most of the world is without Christ and that thousands are dying in their sins every day and going to an endless hell such as the Bible describes. On the other hand they assert that unless someone tells them about Christ so they can "get saved" then thousands more are going to this endless hell every day in the future. In addition they teach that the doctrine of a "second chance" after death is an error. Therefore, theologically speaking, they eternally seal the majority of the billions of the world into the state called hell that the Bible describes very graphically in several passages. After seven years of service as a missionary I was dismissed from the society when I told them that I was unable to go on trying to believe this way.

I have not yet met anyone that acts like they really believe these things. How could they ever laugh or make a joke? How can they have parties and play sports and games?

How can they consume time in social intercourse when all the time they use for these things could be used to contact at least one poor hell-bound soul on the streets of the city in the hope that he just might turn to Christ before he gets killed in a traffic accident, perhaps that very day?

Personally, I have been to the hell that the Bible describes, or at least a reasonable facsimile. God gave me the ability to come back from that hell and I am a different person now because of it. It is an absurdity to say that hell is not at least as bad as my nervous breakdown was. Take a look at the biblical passages describing hell and see for yourself. If I continued to try to believe like my evangelical friends do I would crack up again in a big hurry!

One person asked, "Well Roger, even if hell is not endless why don't you go tell more people about the gospel to keep them from the punishment they would get before they turned to God?" My answer is that God has allowed me to have hope that everyone will be given adequate opportunity to change their wrong attitudes before the extreme measure of the purgings of hell become necessary. Justice demands that they receive this opportunity. Nobody's salvation depends solely on the actions of any one person other than God. My participation or lack of participation in the spreading of the gospel affects only my rewards. It does not affect the destiny of any other person.

God said to the prophet, "Their blood will I require at thy hand, if you don't warn the wicked to turn from their wicked way." I have heard this statement used several times in connection with the torments of hell. It has nothing to do with the torments of hell. It's talking about the physical annihilation of the people. God will see to it that they have adequate opportunity to change their wrong attitudes before the purgings of hell are applied.

Jesus said, "Go ye into all the world and preach the gospel." The gospel is that everyone is already forgiven; they just have to change their attitude to benefit from the forgiveness. God will see to it that before the purgings of hell are used, everyone will have an adequate opportunity to do just that. The eternal destiny of no created being is dependent on the action of any one person other than God Himself. If we fail, He still remains faithful for He cannot deny Himself. Praise God!

As far as my personal responsibility to God is concerned, I am content that I am conducting myself in harmony with God's will for my own personal life day by day. I am the one who has to give an account for the way I conduct my life and I'm prepared to do just that; and I believe it will be based on what I do with the light that God gives me. If my judgment of the light is in error, I hope that God will give me an opportunity to make the appropriate adjustments before He has to bring the purgings of hell to bear upon my soul.

Oswald Chambers said, "Believe what you believe and stick to it. But don't profess to believe more then you intend to stick to." Evangelicals do not conduct themselves in accordance with their beliefs.

Evangelical theology gives us the absurd situation of having the "saved" person up in heaven having a good time, while the person he neglected to introduce to Christ is endlessly suffering the kind of hell that Bible describes, simply because the "saved" person was too lazy to tell them about Christ. Then on top of this absurdity they insist that God is trying His best to save us!

Evangelicals say that at the judgment of Christ every person will agree that every verdict is just. Well, I'm a person, and if any verdict, even that of Satan's, condemns them to an endless hell such as the Bible describes, I will not consider it just!

There are two interpretations of scripture; one is evangelical, the other is total-restorationist. My feelings of security depend on the total-restoration interpretation being right. I hope that hell will be a manifestation of the negative side of God's goodness.

There are two sides to God's goodness, the positive side and the negative side. It is my hope that God can never stop manifesting His goodness to anyone, and that He will keep on manifesting it until every created being is benefitting from the positive side of His goodness. That's just the way God is. That's His essential character. That's what makes Him God!

There are just not enough superlatives to adequately glorify and magnify such a God. What a soul and body relaxing, spirit strengthening concept it is!!!

Some say if hell is not endless why don't we all go out and do as we please and have a good time? I know from experience that they resulting suffering they would ultimately experience as a corrective consequence would make such action undesirable to the least! Beside that, it's my opinion that such a person is not really in love with God and His purposes; they are only lining up because they are afraid of the consequence of not lining up.

I too am afraid of the consequences if I don't line up, but the difference is that God has given me hope that the consequences, horrible as they are, are beneficial rather than eternally destructive. This hope is what gives me the ability to love God rather than having an unhealthy fear of Him.

Asking me to socialize with my evangelical friends without being affected, is like asking me to go into a sepulcher full of rotting bodies and saying, "Pay no attention to the odor, just concentrate on the positive aspects of the tomb."

I have to have a God who is in absolute control all of the time, and who's will that nobody should eternally perish cannot be successfully thwarted. Every gift from God is a good gift, including the gift of a limited free will. If our will were so free that we could choose ourselves into an eternal nightmare, that would not be a good gift. It does despicable despite to the character of God!

I am suffering a divorce from the evangelical system. Many divorced couples love and respect each other from a distance, but there are always certain areas of incompatibility which make close fellowship impossible.

One thing I know experimentally, and that is that for me the secret of victory over bondage of fear is to persist in maintaining an attitude of rejection of many of the beliefs that evangelicals consider "basic." You may wonder how I justify the fact that I work in an evangelical book warehouse. The reason is that 90% of the material is helpful because it avoids doctrine of deals instead with coping with life's various problems. So much good is done by the 90% that I think it outweighs the harm done by the 10%. I think I am making a positive contribution to my country of Canada by helping to dispatch this literature.

You will notice later on that the letter writer "T" insists that at the judgment everyone is going to agree together that the hell that the Bible describes in not only endless, but is absolutely just, so that no one can accuse God of having passed an unjust verdict. I want to repeat what I said before – that I'm going to be there, and I will not approve of such a verdict for anyone!!

Evangelicals have spent their whole lives being taught to interpret every relevant passage of scripture in terms of an endless hell. To reverse this brainwashing process is an enormous task, but I know from experience that it can be done. When you being to see God as I hope He really is, within the perspective of total restoration, then every passage of scripture takes on a brand new dimension and meaning. Scriptures that used to be "problem texts" stand out crystal clear. Theological hassles and seemingly insolvable differences melt away into irrelevancy. The whole Bible takes on the breathtaking scope of magnificent grandure and makes you glad to be alive and a small but important part of the whole plan!

It is my opinion that without the vision of total restoration, nobody can truly love God. Instead of love evangelicals have a very deep gratefulness, much like a child who has managed to control himself from messing his pants when it finally dawns on him that his father is really not going to whip him endlessly.

Evangelicals say that everyone will ultimately agree together that the endless hell concept of "justice" is the right one. Their concept of justice has become so revolting to me that during the last ten years I have experienced a high degree of emotional pain when I have been with them for social purposes. I have managed to maintain a reasonable degree of social poise around them for the sake of my family but it has become increasingly difficult and nerve wracking to do so. I have discovered that my freedom from the bondage of fear, at least for the time being, depends on avoiding social contact with these people. It may be that as the years go by my hope in my new concept of God will become strong enough to displace my intense uncomfortable feelings.

It is impossible for me to understand how any completely sane person does not become intensely disturbed by believing that souls are to suffer endlessly in a hell like the Bible describes; but I have found very little evidence of such disturbance in any evangelicals that I have been acquainted with. The fact that it causes so little disturbance upon their minds makes me wonder if they really are completely in touch with reality! For the language that the Bible uses to describe hell is so graphic that believing that it is endless as well, does not seem to me to be the action of a sane person at all, especially to insist that it is "just."

The only commendable thing that evangelicals have going for them is their desire to "stake everything on the word of God at any cost." The problem is that in this case the cost is too great! When a belief turns the character of God into that of a sadistic fiend, then something must be wrong with the way they are interpreting the Bible. As Abraham Lincoln said to the evangelical evangelist, "Your god is my devil!"

During a conversation with the letter writer "D," he tried to determine if I believed in the "true Jesus Christ" or not. I have to admit quite frankly, that there is such an immeasurable distance between the concept of Jesus Christ that I hope in, and the evangelical concept, that I wonder if we are referring to the same person! I hope that God is so great and wonderful that if any of us are presently involved in a deception that He will turn it into something useful for our benefit and His glory.

Evangelicals have a frantic fear that causes them to consume an enormous amount of energy to attempt to avoid deception at all costs. This causes them to clan together in power structure cells to establish their security by warding off outside influences that try to distract them from believing that their group's way is the only true and right way. As for me, I want to go to hell if that's what God thinks is best for me. Whatever He wants, I want.

This may be true, but it <u>does matter</u> to me what they believe. What they believe is an enormous problem to me. With the concept of "justice" that they adhere to, I can love them from a distance, but their concept is so irrational and insane to me that I cannot feel comfortable when attempting to socialize with them.

Other evangelical friends say, "As long as you love Jesus, that's all that matters to us." My reaction to this is, "Who is Jesus anyway, other than the sum total of His attributes?" – and if creating beings who can choose themselves into an endless hell of torment like the Bible describes is a manifestation of one of His attributes, I simply cannot love Him. I can be scared to the brink of insanity of Him as I have been all my life until recently, but there is <u>no way</u> I can love Jesus if the hell that the Bible describes is endless. Consequently, there is no way that I can feel comfortable around people who believe that Jesus is like evangelicals say He is.

Their condition for accepting me and loving me is, "as long as I love Jesus." I have to have Jesus who accepts me and loves me whether or not I love Him! I have to have a Jesus who will demonstrate even by hell if necessary, that He will never give up on me or stop loving me. I have to have a Jesus whose love is stronger than my free will, and I hope that He will use that strength on everyone and not give up on anyone. I have to have a Jesus who allows torture only for a redemptive purpose. I have to have a Jesus who has a sane and rational concept of justice and will not allow anyone to be tortured endlessly. I have to have a Jesus who will never seal hell shut but will use it to accomplish repentance.

Sealing people into endless torture and crying, "too late, too late" is an absolutely irrational and insane concept of justice!

Evangelicals teach that God grants to everyone only a certain amount of grace, both time-wise and quantity-wise. They say that when the time limit runs out and the soul has used up its quote of grace by hardening itself against the wooing of the Holy Spirit, then that soul has "had it," is "done for," is eternally lost, irrecoverable even by God Himself. They say that they will be sealed into torture in an endless hell. They can give no rational or sane reason for this torture other than it's the "justice" of God, and they persist in maintaining that this concept of justice is rational and sane!

For thirty years I have not loved Jesus Christ, although I pretended to out of fear. It's only during the last ten years following my nervous breakdown that I have begun to love Him. My ability to love Him has been directly related to my ability to successfully reject evangelical theology.

My evangelical friends, I want you to know that I love you, but your beliefs are just <u>too much</u> for me to handle, and I'm sorry to say that I can find no relaxation in your presence no matter how kind and hospitable you are towards me.

This creates a problem for me because my in-laws are evangelical. Fortunately for me, God has allowed my wife to change her evangelical beliefs to that of total restoration, and while I only have hope in it, she actually has faith! Needless to say this has been a great blessing to me!

I work very hard all year long. Nearly all the time, every day, I give 100% of myself in my work. Three weeks of the year are given to me for vacation. During these three weeks I <u>need</u> to relax, but I can't relax among people who believe as they do. These people have <u>faith</u> in the endlessness of hell while I only have <u>hope</u> in total restoration. Faith wins over hope any day, but in winning they have lost me.

They are very nice, kind people most of the time and I wish things were different so I could enjoy myself in their presence.

My wife is a wonderful person! I doubt there are many in this world like her. She was reared in an evangelical atmosphere so it can't be all bad. It shows me that God is using Babylon, for she is a golden cup in the hands of the Lord, but a time is coming when all institutionalized religion will vanish away.

I suppose it's the evidence of how God has used evangelicalism that has made it difficult to break away from their influence – but I am breaking away. It is proving to be a long struggle, BUT I AM BREAKING AWAY!

From my point of view a great deal more of the energy of evangelicalism is being used up on "group kingdom building" rather than building the kingdom of God. It is probably in the areas that they least expect it that evangelicals are being the most effective. Much of the rest is just the product of "group kingdom building."

I would rather live out my life with only hope in total restoration that to have faith in endless suffering. Even if evangelicals did teach a second chance after death, their belief that souls can choose themselves into a hell such as the Bible describes as believe that it never comes to an end, is just too much for me to emotionally handle!

NEVER IN THE HISTORY OF HUMAN EMOTION, HAS THERE BEEN A HATRED MORE PERFECT THAN MINE TOWARDS A DOCTRINE OF THE CHRISTIAN CHURCH!!!

I hope that God is essentially good, even though when I cried out for mercy hour after hour, day after day and month after month during my nervous breakdown, it seemed that He didn't pay any attention to me and only let me get worse and WORSE! Even though I sought help from everyone I could think of there was no help to be found. I hope that He is a good God and will work

I hope that God is essentially good, even though when I cried out for mercy hour after hour, day after day and month after month during my nervous breakdown, it seemed that He didn't pay any attention to me and only let me get worse and WORSE! Even though I sought help from everyone I could think of there was no help to be found. I hope that He is a good God and will work <u>every</u> negative thing out for good for <u>everyone,</u> so it will be better that the negative thing happened than had it not happened.

I believe in hell. Man, do I believe in hell! I'm probably more convinced of the existence of the kind of hell that the Bible describes than most other people in the world.

Ray Prinzing says that since he became a total restorationist he believes in a hotter hell than he ever did before, hot enough in fact to change the minds of the rebellious and cause them to want to come to Christ and have their heart changed.

The rest of my life will demonstrate just how much reality there is in my hope and what it will do for me. The proof of the pudding will be in the eating. I'm content to wait till God's appointed time for me to have faith, and my hope has become strong enough now to not be overwhelmed by the condemnation of the evangelicals – at least from a distance.

One letter writer in this manuscript says that my expressions of hope are "just words." <u>They are much more than "just words" to me</u>! My hopes are the very essence of my life. They make up the very atmosphere in which I live and move and have my being.

For thirty years I lied about having assurance of salvation. For thirty years I lied about having the witness of the Spirit that I was a child of God. I lied in an effort to convince myself and others that it was the truth. The alternative, endless suffering in hell was too emotionally painful for me to face up to. When I finally did face up to it I have a complete nervous breakdown.

My feelings of security concerning life after death are dependent on evangelical theology being wrong. The following pages will help to explain and defend the reasons for the hope that is in me.

Some time has elapsed since writing A DESERT JOURNEY. Immediately after writing it life began to be deliciously rewarding. My hope in the total restoration of all has become stronger.

The desert is fading behind me now. All around me is grassy plain. My senses seem to be sharper. The scenery of nature seems more beautiful, the breezes more balmier and the songs of the birds sweeter. Life in general is becoming more worth living.

The essential result of writing A Desert Journey was the burning of the bridge of access that linked me with evangelicalism. In THE GRASSY PLAIN I will clean up some of the rubble that was caused by the burning of the bridge.

The response to A DESERT JOURNEY from my evangelical friends was just as I had predicted. They cannot accept the fact that my hopes are the solution, not the cause of my fading problem with uncontrollable fear. With the concept of God that I now hope in life is becoming a precious experience. I am beginning to feel like I may be able to survive any crises that may come my way. I sense there is a certain amount of irony in my soul now, and strength in my spirit, and purpose in my heart.

Because of the nature of my hopes I didn't think I needed to become aggressively evangelistic about them. "After all," I said to myself, "the end is secure, so there's nothing at stake if I keep quiet and don't rock the boat." However, I discovered that this attitude was not a good one, for it left me I "never, never land," with most of my evangelical friends thinking I was one way, when really I wasn't anything like they thought I was. I also discovered the harder I sought to defend my hope, the stronger it became, and my bondage to fear became less of a problem proportionately.

Military experts say that very often the best defense is a strong offense. This seems to be true in my case. For ten years I have been fighting the good fight to defend my hope in a concept of God that produces positive rather than negative results within myself. For ten years I have been emotionally and mentally preparing myself for this moment. I now feel ready to enter the battle. God help me!

During the past ten years I have carefully studied the objective evidences and examined and re-examined my personal motives. The responses that I received from my evangelical friends who read A DESERT JOURNEY, gave me strong incentive to reply to their arguments and defend my hope. Although I love them all and harbor no bitterness towards them, I intend to show that their concept of God is a hideously evil and vile concept, and I hope that I will be able to influence people away from it.

I would like the reader now to prayerfully examine the following exchange of letters within the context of what I have already written.

# THE LETTERS

The first letter is from a very good friend of mine. Like myself, he was reared by evangelical parents and educated in an evangelical Sunday School, and like myself he became an agnostic. He is the most well-read person I have ever met and I always find his company immensely relaxing and enjoyable.

C.S. Lewis once said that an honest atheist is more pleasing in the eyes of God than a "Christian" who doesn't live in accordance with their beliefs.

Oswald Chambers once said, "I never met a man who lost his faith in God. Many men have lost their faith in their beliefs and for awhile they think they have lost their faith in God. They have lost the conception which has been presented to them as God, and are coming to God on a new line. It is absurd to tell a man he must believe this and that; in the meantime he can't. Scepticism is produced by telling men what to believe. We get impatient and take men by the scruff of the neck and say, 'You must believe in this and that'. You cannot make a man see moral truth by persuading his intellect. Truth is always a vision that arises in the basis of the moral nature, never in the intellect. Jesus put the disciples through crises to revel them to themselves and bring them to the place of receiving the truth."

Oswald Chambers also said, "We begin our religious life by believing our beliefs, we accept what we are taught without questioning; but when we come up against things we begin to be critical, and find out that the beliefs are not right for us because we have not bought them by suffering. What we take for granted is never ours until we have bought is by pain. A thing is worth just what it costs. The natural virtues in some people are charming and delightful, but let a presentation of truth be given that they have not seen before, and there is an exhibition of the most extraordinary resentment, proving that all their piety was purely temperamental".

And one more thing from Oswald Chambers: "NEVER ACCEPT AN EXPLANATION OF ANY OF GOD'S WAYS WHICH INVOLVES WHAT YOU WOULD SCORN AS UNFAIR AS A MAN".

I present to you now the letter of my friend.

Dear Roger:

I feel a bit of an ass for not writing some sort of reply to your manuscript which I received a few weeks ago. It's amazing how time can go so fast and yet so infernally slow at the same time. I have been trying to write something appropriate ever since I read your open letter. I keep going off on tangents which, as I say, are inappropriate.

The fact is that, as an agnostic, there isn't very much for me to say, except that I'm glad that you have, as it seems, resolved your inner conflicts regarding eternal hell, or at least you are well on your way to solving them.

I might add that our experiences with the evangelicals have been to some extent similar in that we have both found their teachings to be life-negating. That we differ from that point on can be rather poignantly expressed by saying that Bertrand Russell is to me as Ray Prinzing is to you. Psychology, rather than religion, is still the basis of my approach to solving the problems of the human condition. (Which is not to say that I go around trying to solve other people's problems – I find my own sufficiently exhausting, though not particularly interesting.)

I have been trying to 'get it together' to write a sort of statement concerning my own beliefs (or rather lack of them) and their formation, but I find it difficult to organize it into a coherent and readable form. So far it's quite unreadable: page after page of unspeakable rubbish – indicating, I think, quite accurately the present state of my mental processes. If I ever get it sorted out and properly expurgated, I'll send you a copy. You may find it entertaining if not edifying.

In conclusion, let me congratulate you for having come through a very difficult period made all the harder, as it seems to me, by the emotional needs of some of your Christian friends, who evidently found you an easy scape goat for their own fears and uncertainties. May your journey continue to be life-affirming rather than life-denying.

Sincerely Phil

PS: I have included excerpts from Tennyson's IN MEMORIUM in which he seems to express some of your own anxieties concerning man's destiny – Also some of your hopes and mine.

Strong Son of God, Immortal Love,
Who we, that have not seen Thy face
By faith and faith alone embrace,
Believing where we cannot prove;

Thine are these orbs of light and shade;
Thou madest life in man and brute.
Thou madest death; and lo, Thy foot
Is on the skull which Thou hast made.

Thou wilt not leave us in the dust;
Thou madest man, he knows not why;
He thinks he was not made to die;
And Thou hast made him: Thou art just.

Thou seemest human and divine,
The highest , holiest manhood, Thou,
Our wills are ours, we know not how;
Our will are ours, to make them Thine.

We have but faith; we cannot know;
For knowledge is of things we see,
And yet we trust it comes from Thee,
A beam in darkness: let it grow.

Forgive these wild and wandering cries
Confusions of a wasted youth;
Forgive them where they fail in truth,
And in Thy wisdom make me wise.

Be near me when the sensuous frame
Is racked with pangs that conquer trust;
And time, a maniac scattering dust,
And life a fury slinging flame.

Be near me when my faith is dry
And men the flies of latter Spring,
That lay their eggs and sting and sting
And weave their petty cells and die.

O yet we trust that somehow good
Will be the final goal of ill,
To pangs of nature, sins of will,
Defects of doubt, and taints of blood;

That nothing walks with aimless feet;
That not one life will be destroyed,
Or cast as rubbish to the void
When God hath made the pile complete.

That not a worm is cloven in vain;
That not a moth with vain desire
Is shriveled in a fruitless fire,
Or but subserves another's gain.

Behold we know not anything;
I can but trust that good shall fall
At last – far off – at last, to all
And every winter change to Spring.

So runs my dreams; but what am I?
An infant crying in the night;
An infant crying for the light;
And with no language but a cry.

Note: I received more help from this poem sent to me by an agnostic than I received from any of the replies from my evangelical friends.

I would like to have had Tennyson for a friend. I think we might have been very compatible. I was pleased to see that God granted him faith. I long for the day when my hope evolves into faith!

Nothing fake about Tennyson is there? – I feel he was speaking from the very bottom of his soul. Great stuff!!

The following letter is from an older lady who has spent much of her life introducing hundreds of children to Jesus Christ.

Roger Dear:

How I love you! (Except I should say I hate you, for the whole morning has passed in reading your Journey and my dusting is still not done!) I love you for having put into words all the things you had in your heart, and have openly declared your beliefs.

For some time now I too have been so disillusioned with the evangelicals, who have made some of the declarations which you have brought out in the open, and even though this letter is not going to be long, please believe me dear one …. I am with you all the way.

You, Helen and the children are four of my most precious possessions.

I love you all!

> Dede

Note: The following several hundred pages show that I had not yet "put into words all the things that I had in my heart! "This lady has been a solid rock for my anchor during an exceedingly stormy tempest. I am grateful to God for her presence in my life.

The following short note emphasizes the contrast between the several kinds of reactions to my DESERT JOURNEY manuscript.

Dear Roger:

Thanks for the fine manuscript. Praise God for your emancipating process.

I am sure that God who began the good work within you will keep on helping you grow in His grace until His task within you is finally finished.

Love you lots.

> Andy

The following letter is from my mother-in-law, a fine, sincere and dedicated lady. I deeply regret that much of my emotional pain has been, and still is caused by the fact that my in-laws are involved in a theology which has caused the only <u>serious</u> problem that I have ever had in my life.  All my in-laws are fine people but I simply cannot emotionally cope with what they believe. They have <u>faith</u> in their concept of God; I only have <u>hope</u> in mine. And the two concepts are an infinite distance apart. God may yet allow my hope in my concept to become strong enough to be able to enjoy fellowship with them again, but this is not in the foreseeable future.

The fact that they are so loving and kind has only complicated my problem and made it all the more difficult to break free from their theology which I tried so hard to believe for the first thirty years of my life, but which finally caused my nervous breakdown.

Dear Roger and Helen:

We were so glad for your manuscript Roger. Even if it isn't all a happy situation, I think it is so good to be able to tell it like it is. I'm so glad we are on that good a sharing basis. I am certain in my own heart and spirit that God is in the process of doing a lot of internal healing in our whole family. Sometimes we hardly know where the hurt is coming from, but <u>He</u> does, and He will show us.

I love you Roger, just the way it is and I truly think you are a very nice person, a very kind person; intelligent, vital, careful, polite, faithful, and I could use a lot more adjectives too, all along the same line. Besides loving you, I think you're great! – and that comes straight from my heart.

Love you all.

Mom and Dad

Here is a second letter from her:

Roger, we are rejoicing about the news in your letter – great! – Praise the Lord – What a relief for you. I'm excited about what God is doing in all our families.

It's so wonderful that you have faith and joy back Roger. We are happy, happy – joyful. Perhaps times of joy are expressed better on the face than by the pen.

Love to you all.

Mom and Dad

Dear Mom and Dad:

I have deeply appreciated all the positive things that you have said in your letters to Helen and I. They have meant so very much to me!

When you receive a copy of THROUGH THE DESERT TO THE GRASSY PLAIN you will disagree with many things. Many things will sound harsh to you and may even hurt you, although hurting you is not my intention.

There is a very real possibility that I will never be coming to see you again. After you read my book you will understand why.

Joy is expressed better on the face than by the pen, but sometimes a certain problem causes one to not show his joyful face. When you read my complete manuscript you will understand what I mean.

Love,

    Roger

The psychological force of an evangelical power cell is enormous. When a group has an opinion about what is God's will for a certain individual, it is practically impossible for that person not to conform to it. Even though that person might leave the group for several years and rebel against what the group thinks is God's will for him, still, in the end he will likely return and submit.

Such is the case with the former husband of the next letter writer. He is now back in what the group calls "the centre of God's will." But yielding to this pressure from the group was at least partially responsible for the termination of his marriage.

Dear Roger:

You don't really know me, as we've met only once a few years ago. I do not mean to intrude. I am writing this solely from honest concern for you and your endless hell friends.

I also believe that hell is endless, but I can see your point that a truly loving God would not send His children to torment forever. He doesn't want to, so He gave us Jesus.

I believe from your story that you love the Lord and I can't imagine Him not loving you, although because you are suffering, it seems He's forsaken you.

You say you must not be in Christ because "there is no condemnation to those in Christ". That quote means, those who believe in Christ are free from sin and death; their life will be eternal, even though they may suffer here on earth. The Bible also says than many will suffer in His name, but Christ will remember them in the judgment day. This suffering isn't always the result of defending Jesus to pagans, but simply trying to live a good life amidst those whose beliefs demand more than Jesus asks of you to be saved.

Your manuscript makes me sad. Sad, because the people who try to help you should do it expressing love not doctrine. However I don't condemn them as I don't have all the answers and I know their motives are good.

Love is the basis of all God's work and the reason to do God's work. It seems that all you life people have taught you to fear – fear God – fear God – etc. I believe one must do things out of love to be sincere. People who try to instill fear are wrong because they teach an "you must do it this way or else" attitude, which is not something out of one's own will, but because he is afraid of the consequences. God wants you to love Him of your free will, not out of fear, or He wouldn't have given us a choice.

I know how hard it can be to convince people of your love for God when your beliefs differ. It's not necessary for them to believe you. Only God must, and will because He knows everything in your heart. He knows that you are trying and He knows the good that you are doing.

Not everyone's the same and we can't try to be something we're not. So if you believe you are keeping God's word and you believe you are not sinning, be strong in that. God knows and you know. God won't condemn you.

We're all sinners and we repent, only sometimes to sin again, but each time we ask His forgiveness, He forgives us and the path is clear to heaven, so long as we are sincere. Those who suffer most on earth shall be first in heaven. "The last shall be first, and the first last".

Hell without end is not the basis of Christianity. Eternal life in heaven is, so dwell on that.

You're gonna make it there Roger, I know you are! God is love! It's only some religions that have made Him to fear. Don't fear Ted! It will be yours. It has to be, as you are trying very hard to do what is right. All you can do is try. Nothing more than that can be asked of you. Did you know that if you sinned all your life and on your death bed, you asked sincere forgiveness, God would bring you to heaven? I believe that. He is forgiving. I wouldn't want to live my life in sin and then wait for my death to ask forgiveness, as I feel I wouldn't deserve it, but God would forgive. It's never too late for Him.

You are living a good life by shunning evil, teaching your children of Christ, reading about the Lord and doing your best to be righteous. Isn't that all God asks?!

I like your idea of loving people, not on the basis of whether they've been saved or not, but just because they are people. You are a special person to recognize and utilize the simple principle from the Bible that to love everyone, means exactly that!

I'm not writing this to push my beliefs on you. Everyone must find what makes him happy, so long as that happiness doesn't depend on hurting others.

Roger, I'm happy you've found peace. After I read your manuscript in its entirety, I realize perhaps my letter to you is not necessary. But I'm sending it anyway to let you know that there is someone who believes in some ways the same as you, and that someone is glad that you have found what is right for you. Let no one take it away.

Divine love always has met, and always will meet every human need.

With love.

    Claudia

The most remarkable thing about this last letter is that although Claudia is an endless hell person, still she recognized from reading A DESERT JOURNEY that I found a measure of deliverance. What a stark contrast this letter is from the letters by "T" and "D" which are to follow later. Because they are unable to approve of the way I am finding deliverance, they wrote as though I was still right in the middle of my problem.

The following is my reply to Claudia:

Dear Claudia:

Thank you for your kind letter that I received today. I am pleased that even though you do not know me, yet you wanted to try to help me.

I think I am better than 90% right when I say that we are all victims of the theological system to which we have been exposed from our childhood on. For instance, if I was born into a Roman Catholic family, an evangelical family, a restorationist family, a Jewish family or a Muslim family, there would be a better than 90% chance that I would live out my life and die in that same persuasion.

Only a traumatic experience such as I went through would serve to jolt one from the "true way" which is what each persuasion thinks about themselves.

Speaking purely from a natural point of view, if I had my life to live over, I would like to be born into a total restorationist family, attend the Pittsburgh Bible Institute (a total restoration Bible school), and marry into a total restorationist family.

I can appreciate the frustration the total restorationist student must have experienced when he was asked to leave the evangelical Bible school from which I graduated. I really don't understand why he would even bother to apply in the first place.

I would be pleased to have you read THROUGH THE DESERT TO THE GRASSY PLAIN when I send it to your relatives. Because I don't even know you, I'm not even going to try to respond to the various things you said. When you read my next effort you will easily understand from it what my response would have been had I known you better.

I do know from your letter, that you wanted to try to help me, and this I can tell you, I appreciated very much.

Sincerely,

Roger

Another note from my wife's folks:

Dear Roger:

We are glad to have you say you don't intend to hurt us, and we are glad you are learning many things by putting your thoughts in writing.

We love you Roger! Never mind anything else.

Mom and Dad

Dear Mom and Dad:

Thanks for the letter we received from you today.

The fact that you mentioned the possibility of "hurt" from my forthcoming manuscript causes me to want to assure you that none of the things I have written spring from bitterness in my heart.

By writing, I am establishing my true personal identity and declaring to everyone, "This is me, like it or not." I am finding that there is strong therapeutic value in writing down things as they are from my point of view. Instead of trying to fake my way through the rest of my life, I am letting you know what I am really like.

The hurt that you referred to in your letter may have been the hurt that I have already caused. I sincerely apologize for any hurt that I have already caused.

What we have going between you folk and myself is similar to a married couple's quarrel. We are closer to a "divorce" than you might realize.

For ten years I have suffered like I hope you never suffer. Now I am asking you to suffer with me as in my book I try to explain to you why I find it impossible to enjoy your company.

I know that you both love me, and it means a lot to me to read it in words. You can't repeat it too often, especially through this particularly difficult period of time. I hope that your love will be strong enough to hold up under the impact of finding out why I am unable to emotionally cope with what you people believe.

Love.

Roger

PS: Even many divorced folk still love each other!

The following letter is very important. From 1958 – 68, I respected the author of this letter above all other men. By being able to respond the way I did, I discovered that I became more free than I ever had been before from evangelical bondage.

Dear Roger:

I read THE DESERT JOURNEY last night. I, of course, read your open letter some time ago and answered it; but now I have read the whole story. I never knew how much you had suffered. Our hearts go out to you, and we would really like to help you, but it is difficult to find our way into your mind so that you will really understand what we want to say.

I want to thank you for your very kind words about us. I am sorry however, that we never have been able to be of that help that we want to be and that you really need.

Since I read your paper last night, I would like to say something. Knowing more of the torture you have been going through, I want to assure you of our love. We are deeply stirred and concerned. We don't want you to suffer like that one minute more.

There are certain things that come to me that I really feel I should share with you. First of all, I believe you should not equate your nervous breakdown and the sufferings then and since with hell. You believe that is what hell is. We use the expression "hell" to describe disagreeable and painful experiences. There are also certain figures used in scripture such as fire, etc. that should not be taken literally.

Editor's Note: ( I want to pause here awhile because this is a key issue. Later in this letter, the writer says to me, "The reason you don't have faith is because you don't believe the Bible."

If he himself really believed the Bible he wouldn't make the ridiculous assertion that hell is not as bad as a nervous breakdown.

He also said that people will choose to stay in hell rather than submit to Christ. While on vacation at the Bible school where this letter writer lives a student made the same statement to my then eight year old son.

In order to emphasize the complete absurdity of such a statement I have compiled some of the Biblical references about hell. Although the "fire" may not be literal, there should be no question whatsoever to an objective reader's mind that hell is at least as bad as a nervous breakdown.

Over and over again throughout my life I have heard evangelicals declare with great emphasis that the Bible is the word of God but when they encounter a difficult passage that doesn't conform to their preconceived theology, they simply refuse to accept it for what it actually says. THE DOCTRINE OF HELL IS THE BEST OF ALL THE EXAMPLES OF THIS HYPOCRISY!

Here is what the Bible says about hell.

Matthew 13:42 & 50 – "furnace of fire," "wailing and gnashing of teeth."

Luke 16: 23 & 24 – "and in hell . . . being in torment . . . he cried 'Have mercy on me and send Lazarus that he may dip the tip of his finger in water, and cool my tongue; for I am in torment in this flame'."

Revelation 14: 10 & 11 – "tormented with fire and brimstone – no rest day or night."

Revelation 20: 10, 14 & 15 – "lake of fire – tormented day and night."

This is not as bad as a nervous breakdown?! People will actually rather stay in this place instead of submitting to their Creator, the source of all blessing?! God will actually let them want to suffer like this – eternally?!

When this letter writer submitted this "solution" to my problem, I lost some of the respect that I used to have for him.

If God were to allow people to actually want to stay forever in this Biblical hell, then He surely must be the most heinous fiend that ever existed! And my strongest hope would be that there is a more powerful God out there somewhere that would reveal Himself and overthrow this other God who allows His created beings to want to suffer endlessly.

In GOSPEL ECHOES #598, Ray Prinzing says, "Ask the vast majority of Christian workers what the purpose and way of God is for man today, and they might tell you that it is to "get souls saved" and proceed to quote you John 3:16.

But should you be so bold as to state that this is true, that God so loved the world that He gave His Son for the world, that the world through Him might be saved, and they will immediately tell you that is "false doctrine," that God will not save the whole world, only those who "get saved, and believe as they in their church do." Blind to the ways and purposes of God, they cannot instruct others in comprehensive insight, so they simply parrot the traditions of man.

But how little do they know of the WAY OF THE CROSS, the way into nothingness that He might become everything; they way into losing all your trite and meaningless answers, so that you might BECOME THE ANSWER."

I continue with the letter from "T") –

There is punishment and separation we know. The Bible makes it plain that no one needs to go there that doesn't want to.

Editor's Note: Can you imagine anyone actually wanting to go to the place described at the top of this page?!

I continue with the letter from "T" –

Someone has said that he devil would rather reign in hell than submit to God in heaven, and I suppose that is the attitude of those who refuse to yield to the drawing power of the love of God.

You make it plain that you don't want to turn your back on God, and you don't want to refuse His righteousness. You seem to make it plain that you have chosen to submit to God's righteousness. We become righteous by faith and not by self effort. We choose to live according to the ways of God and as we do, so He gives us the power that is needed.

Universalism, I believe is error, but it is error that one can hold and still be a submitted Christian. One is not lost by believing that error. (Editor's note: The evangelical definition of "lost" is endless hell.)

The last time I talked with Hannah Hurnard, she held firmly to the doctrine of the universalists. At the same time, she believed in Jesus Christ as her Lord and Savior and seemed to be living in vital fellowship with Him. But then she began to add other errors such as reincarnation (not the Hindu kind of endless rebirths.) She told me personally that she did believe in several reincarnations.

In your paper you mention several times that you are not an evangelical. Then you give your statement of faith. You repeatedly state that you hope, but don't have faith, but that you wish you had faith. You also say that when I told you to trust the Lord, it was like telling a cripple to walk. But Jesus did exactly that. You remember the man with the withered hand. He said, "Stretch out your hand." Several times He told people after they had been healed, "Your faith has made you whole." Faith links man with omnipotence and that produces results.

Editor's Note: He only quoted part of my statement. My whole statement was, "It was like telling a cripple to walk WITHOUT IMPARTING THE POWER TO MAKE HIS FAITH OPERATIVE."

This letter writer "T" is condemning me for not exercising faith. The plain fact is that I don't have any faith. "T" cannot accept this. He maintains that I do have faith but I'm just not using it. His attitude has caused me to lost even more of the respect that I used to have for him.

THERE IS NO WAY THAT I CAN EXERCISE FAITH IN A GOD WHO ALLOWS HIS CREATED BEINGS TO ACTUALLY WANT TO LIVE IN A HELL LIKE THE BIBLE DESCRIBES AND NEVER BE ABLE TO GET OUT OF IT.

It's a marvel to me that there are not more evangelicals having nervous breakdowns than there are! Surely it is only the grace of God that is keeping them from flying apart emotionally and mentally! <u>That any such doctrine should be considered credible is by far the greatest mystery of all time</u>.

I continue with the letter from "T" –

God would never command us to do anything we could not do. Therefore, since He commands us to repent, we can repent. Since He commands us to believe – we can believe – we can have faith. Jesus said in John 15:5, "Apart from me you can do nothing." That is the truth of course. But a Christian is not apart from Christ. Jesus lives in a believer. Therefore, with Paul we can say, "I can do all things through Him who strengthens me." Jesus also said, " Greater is He that is in you that he that is in the world." Therefore, if Jesus lives in us, we have the power in us to do what he wants us to.

Editor's note: It is my hope that nowhere in the Bible does God command us to believe in a god who allows his created beings to endlessly want to suffer the kind of hell that the Bible itself describes.

I, Roger Tutt, have no assurance that God lives in me, except through my hope that He will sooner or later live in everyone. I think He is already living in <u>everyone</u>. If He's not I hope that He ultimately will be.

It wasn't so very long ago that this last paragraph from "T" might well have caused my suicide. I would have been forced to conclude that not only was Jesus not within me, but that He had completely forsaken me altogether. Fortunately my respect for the words that come from this particular writer have been reduced to the classification of an opinion, rather than the very word of God.

I still respect a "Christian's" right to have their own opinion, and I respect their need to stand by their own convictions, but I have lost nearly all other respect I have for "Christians."

I continue with the letter from "T" –

You say you have hope, not faith. I am glad to read over and over again about your attitude towards Jesus Christ. You don't want to resist or reject Him. You find it hard to believe in God because you have misconceptions about the character of God.

Editor's Note: I think it is "T" who has the misconception about God's character!

I continue with the letter from "T" –

Luther had that problem. He was terribly disturbed and under deep conviction. His superior tried to help him but he said, "My sin is unforgivable." His superior mentioned certain sins and said that even if he committed those, he still could be forgiven. Luther said, " You don't understand."

"Then what is your problem?" asked his superior. "I do not love God and I know that is unforgivable" said Luther. He only knew God as a stern, uncompromising judge. He had not yet come into an understanding of what God is really like.

God is like the father of the prodigal – loving, waiting, longing for him to return. Our God has done everything He possibly could to make us want to come to Him. The one thing he will not do, and perhaps cannot do, is to violate our free wills.

Editor's note: This last statement is the heart and root, the very essence of the foundation upon which the great and horrible error of evangelical theology is laid. There is absolutely nothing that I disagree with more strongly! I have more to say about this later.

I continue with the letter from "T" –

God has demonstrated His love for us in thousands of ways – especially on Calvary's cross – trying to draw us to Himself.

Editor's note: This last statement is pathetic! Here we have a god who is trying so very hard to get us to respond to his love, but in the end he may only be able to convince a few that his love is worth responding to, and the rest of us he will cast into a hell like the Bible describes and never let us out!

I continue with the letter from "T" –

If we refuse His love, I suppose He will allow certain things to happen, but He will not force us. Since we are made in His image, we do have free wills. If He forces us to do something – that is if He violates our free will – that action would not be a moral action. Therefore there would neither be reward or punishment for it.

Editor's note: "No reward or punishment"??!! You mean to say that our "free will" is more important than saving people from the endless hell that the Bible describes? What an utterly horrible concept of God!

It Is my sincere hope that although God will not violate our free will HE WILL INDEED MAKE US WILLING to choose the right way. I have more to say about this later.

I continue with the letter from "T" –

You speak so often of the endless hell people as if that is our major doctrine. (Editor's note: I intend to show that it is their major doctrine.)

Hell is rarely mentioned in our sermons here. We do not use that method to scare people into the kingdom of God. If we only got people to turn to God through fear, I doubt they would remain faithful. (Editor's note: I intend to show that fear is indeed the basic motivating force that causes people to enter and stay in what evangelicals call "the kingdom of God.")

I continue with the letter from ""T" –

There are two great forces in the world. One is fear and the other is faith. Faith is stronger. As I said before, God will never command us to do anything we cannot do. He does command us to repent and believe. Therefore, we can do both.

Editor's Note: I agree that we can believe, if what we are asked to believe is compatible with a just and righteous concept of the character of God. Evangelicals do not have a just and righteous concept of the character of God.

Love is a greater force than either fear or faith. It NEVER fails! Love will not allow anyone to suffer endlessly.

I continue with the letter from "T" –

You have hope, not faith. The reason you have hope and not faith is that you don't believe the Bible. "Faith cometh by hearing, and hearing by the word of God." If we make up our own statement of faith, we can only hope because we have nothing really to base it on which is absolutely unchangeable and unshakable. But since you don't believe the Bible – only your own conclusions – you will never have faith, only hope. (Editor's note: "T" doesn't believe the Bible either; he only believes his interpretation of the Bible, as also do I.)

At the same time you have such a high regard for God and His Son, Jesus Christ, that you have not renounced Him, and you don't want to. Therefore it seems that you belong to Him. If it were not for that you would have renounced and turned from Him long ago.

You find it hard to love Him. You are in the same position that Luther was in. But Luther discovered that God was not only a judge but a loving Heavenly Father who sent His Son to redeem us. When Luther saw God as He really was, He found that he could and did love Him. As a result he brought in the reformation. (Editor's note: When I, through hope, see God as He really is, I find that I can love Him too. But I cannot love a god who allows his created beings to suffer endlessly.)

There may be some things in the Bible we don't understand, but the Bible says, "God is love." He has proved His love and keeps on proving it. He is not the author of your torture.

Editor's Note: This last statement is a serious error and it caused me to lose even more respect for "T." Even Job's afflictions were from God. The instrument God used was Satan, BUT THEY WERE FROM GOD. I have considerably more to say about this later one.

I continue with the letter from "T" –

I wouldn't say that the devil is the author of your torture either, (at least not directly so.) We don't see the devil and demons in everything. (Editor's note: During the three years that I was with this group it was my observation that they did in fact "see demons" in <u>almost every</u> negative thing.)

I continue with the letter from "T" –

We know that wrong thinking can cause all kinds of sickness, pain and suffering. Right thinking on the other hand causes health, peace and joy. Right thinking, of course, includes right thinking about God. (Editor's note: It is interesting to note that I am at long last beginning to find peace by rejecting evangelical's so-called "right thinking." "T" would strongly disagree with such a method of finding peace!)

We can hope that things turn out alright, but if we have something absolutely infallible to base our hope on, then we can know that everything will turn out alright. Instead of hope we can have faith. I can't believe things are incompatible. (Editor's note: I wonder then how "T" can believe that God is loving and just and at the same time He allows his created being to choose themselves into a hell like the Bible describes and leaves them there eternally? There is nothing in the whole universe what is more incompatible than these two assertions!)

I can't believe the world is square or flat. I can't believe it is impossible to please God and that God will punish us because we don't please Him. Would a man put a 100 pound weight on a small boy and then whip him for not being able to carry it? Would that be love or justice? Of course not. Our God is not like that. He will never punish us for anything we cannot do. God is a just God, and whatever His punishment might be, it will be suited to the crime. God is a redeeming God, and His desire is to save us, to transform us and make us like Jesus Christ.

In some places you refer to God's sovereignty in such a manner that He will have His way with us whether we will it or not. (Editor's note: I lost some more respect for "T" because of this last statement. Let the reader go back and read my previous words. Never did I say that God would force us against our will. What I did say was that God will make us willing to choose His way. There's a big difference!)

He will never violate our free will but He will do everything He possibly can to win us to Himself. (Editor's note: Another pathetic statement! I have my hope in a God who will be successful in causing us to want to will His will. It is not possible for me to feel secure with a concept of God like the one "T" has. For 28 years I tried to find feelings of security by trying to love and trust the evangelical God. All I finally got out of it was a nervous breakdown, and a lot of increasingly severe emotional pain throughout the years before my breakdown. How great must be the grace of God that allows "T" to believe such nonsense and yet prospers him abundantly at the same time!)

I continue with the letter from "T" –

I do not believe God is the creator of your torture. It is not producing the right results anyway. (Editor's note: Because of my torture there is <u>no way</u> that I will ever rebel against God, at least not intentionally. What results could be more right than that? I know from experience that the Bible is not exaggerating with its description of hell, and I know that nobody who experiences suffering of this intensity would ever again deliberately rebel against God.)

God's sovereignty does not mean He has everything the way He wants it now, but He's going to have everything the way He wants it. I don't know all that means. (Editor's note: I hope it doesn't mean that he will want anyone to suffer endlessly!)

It seems that there are two kingdoms – the kingdom of God and the kingdom of those who refuse to yield to Him. We must not accept the medieval idea about God – that He is a judge only, and almost delights in casting men into an endless hell. (Editor's note: Ray Prinzing says that the dual kingdom theology, one eternally evil versus one eternally good is neither right nor scriptural. I hope he's right. My feelings of security depend on my hope that he is right. Any assurance of salvation that I have is inseparably connected to my hope that nobody will have to suffer endlessly.)

Long ago I settled the issue of knowing that God is love and that He is just. I don't understand everything at the present time, but I know He will do everything just right, and there will be no one to criticize Him. Even those who refuse to yield will admit that He is right. If they continue in the rival kingdom, it is because they want to be there, not simply because of some mistakes they made. They knowingly, voluntarily have chosen not to submit to God. What that kingdom will be like, I don't know. How many will be there, I don't know. God hasn't made it plain. (Editor's note: It is apparent to me that "T" has never experienced the intensity of suffering that the Bible describes as hell. If he had he would never have written this last paragraph. Nobody can suffer like that and function in opposition against God at the same time. It's an impossibility. Such a person is too overwhelmed by their suffering to even think about functioning in opposition to God. It's amazing to me how "T" completely ignores the scriptural description of eternal hell and makes up his own ideas about what it's like. He does the very thing he accuses me of doing when I wrote my statement of hope at the end of A DESERT JOURNEY.)

I continue with the letter from "T" –

He has made plain His love, His willingness to forgive and forget, His willingness to make whole, to give peace, to fill with joy unspeakable that no man can take from us. We major on these positive things we know, and as we do so, more and more people are coming into the kingdom.

Editor's Note: In the pages ahead I intend to show that evangelicals believe that evangelicalism and the kingdom of God are synonymous; and that evangelicalism is part of religious Babylon with each of the 200-plus sections babbling amongst each other in total confusion.

For the time being God is using Babylon; she is a "golden cup in the hands of the Lord." But Babylon (institutionalized religion) will ultimately be destroyed and only the pure kingdom of God will remain.)

I continue with the letter from "T" –

Again, God is not the cause of your torture. (Editor's note: And again I say he is dead wrong!) Demons, perhaps could torture, but in your case, I don't believe they are to be blamed. I believe it is your own thinking. (Editor's note: That's why I am changing my thinking away from the kind of thinking that "T" does, and to the degree that I am being successful in rejecting evangelical thinking, to that degree I am not experiencing any more torture.)

You want to believe the restoration people, but you are not able to believe them completely. They have elements that you missed in your wrong conception of God. This seems to bring some hope, but you are not able to completely forsake the Bible as the infallible word of God. Therefore you are caught between two opinions. (Editor's Note: The fact is that I'm not able to <u>believe</u> anything, but God is allowing me to have a degree of <u>hope</u> that is changing my life. I hope it's "T" who has the wrong conception of God, not me. To the degree that I am able to completely forsake <u>his interpretation</u> of the Bible, to that degree I am being delivered from bondage to fear.)

Again I plead with you – believe that God is love. Everything else about Him has to be consistent with His total love. (Editor's note: - God is love? He allows His created beings to suffer endlessly in the place that the Bible describes as hell – and we are supposed to believe that He is love?! It staggers my mind and emotions!)

He commands us to repent, He commands us to believe; therefore we are able to. You are hoping in your own statement of faith, but you have nothing, really to base it on except your own concepts. We base our faith on the infallible, inerrant Word of God, which reveals God as lovely, wonderful and altogether desirable that we love Him with all our hearts and trust Him not only with our souls, but to do all things right. We want to serve him forever. (Editor's note: "T" believes that <u>his interpretation</u> of the

Bible is infallible and inerrant. I intend to expand on this statement later. How great must be the grace of God that allows "T" to love Him so much in spite of his evangelical theology - or is it really true love that he has for God? I also will discuss this later.)

I continue with the letter from "T" –

We covet for you that peace and joy that comes by trusting God and His word. This is written in love and faith with prayer. May the grace of the Lord Jesus Christ, the love of God and the fellowship of the Holy Spirit be yours. May He deliver you from all wrong thinking, keep you and give you this peace now and forevermore.

Yours in this wonderful Lord

Editor's Note:

Oswald Chambers said, "Faith is a terrific venture in the dark; I have to believe that God is good in spite of all that contradicts it in my experience. It is not easy to say God is love when everything that happens actually gives the lie to it. One of the most curious phases today is that people are expecting Satan to do things. Let us keep our eyes on God and remember that behind the devils is God."

As this point in time I don't see myself as having any faith; nor do I have the ability to exercise faith. But I am very grateful to God for the measure of hope that He has allowed me to have. It is very real and it is working good results in my life.

I know that the Bible says that whatever is not of faith is sin, and without faith it is impossible to please God. I'm not going to try to excuse myself or try to figure out why I don't have faith. Neither am I going to pretend that I have faith as I did for the first 28 years of my life. I pretended because I was not able to emotionally cope with my inability to please God by exercising faith. I pretended in an effort to prevent God from sending me to an endless hell of torment such as the Bible describes.

It is my hope that God will grant me faith according to His time-table.

I'm sure that the motive behind the letter from "T" was pure. BUT THE SOLUTIONS HE OFFERED ME ARE COMPLETELY UNACCEPTABLE AND UNWORKABLE. I'm sure that God will give him an A+ for effort.

The following is my answer to "T." Upon rewriting it years later I find that my hope has become strong enough to face up to the fact that this letter is a gross exaggeration to say the least. It may be more accurate to call it a bare-faced lie. If the word "faith" in this letter were changed to "hope," then the contents of the letter would be closer to the truth.

It's not hard for me to understand why I lied. I had just received a letter from the man who for ten years I respected above all other men and this letter was supposed to contain the solution to my problem with fear and my inability to love and trust God. I was reacting out of fear – fear that what he was saying might be true. The lie was my inner soul screaming, "I don't care how much I respected you in the past, what you are saying to me just cannot be so – for the sake of my mental, emotional and spiritual well being IT CANNOT BE!"

It was false for me to say that my fear was gone. It would have been more accurate for me to say, "My fear is subsiding." The reader should take into account that a lot of water has passed under the bridge since I wrote this letter.

Here then is my reply to "T" –

Dear "T":

Since writing A DESERT JOURNEY I have listened to Ray Prinzing's tape called KEPT IN PEACE and read Hannah Hurnard's THE SECRET OF A TRANSFORMED LIFE. My fear is gone! Faith and joy have returned!

I am further comforted by your expression of love and concern. Although I disagree with nearly everything you said, I cannot miss the obvious good will you are showering upon me and I accept it with gratefulness. It warms my heart and soul, and I want you to know that no matter how much I may disagree with you, I shall always love you for no one could ever persuade me that your heart is not right.

It is impossible for me not to equate my suffering with hell, for the Bible's description of hell fits what I went through. Ray Prinzing points out that <u>nowhere</u> does the Bible say that hell is separation from God. I know from experience that it is possible to have the sun shining, soft breezes blowing, soft fluffy clouds in the sky, the birds singing sweetly and everything outwardly perfect, and yet be in the worst kind of hell imaginable, inwardly.

It's true there will be no sin committed in heaven because when one attempts to express themselves in a sinful way, the hell that they will suffer within will both prevent them from doing it and also condition them so they will not be so likely to try it in the future. NOBODY WOULD RATHER REIGN IN THE HELL THAT THE BIBLE DESCRIBES than to submit to God in heaven. God will not snuff out even the tiniest response towards Him by sticking the person in a hell like the Bible describes.

That Universalism and Reincarnation and my own personal beliefs are error, I recognize as just an opinion and nothing more. No one believes that the Bible is the word of God! However, thousands of people believe that their interpretation of the Bible is the word of God.

The faith that has been restored to me is not faith in the Bible being the word of God, but rather, faith in the essential goodness of God. However, my statement of personal belief does not contradict my interpretation of the "word of God." The peace and joy that I experience when I testify to my faith in my interpretation of the Bible is very real to me.

I don't agree with you that the reason I lack faith is because I don't believe the Bible is the word of God. Like I said before, nobody believes that the Bible is the word of God. Even I believe that my interpretation of the Bible is the word of God!

I don't believe that God is commanding me to exercise faith in your group's interpretation of scripture. I don't recognize your interpretation as being the word of God.

I think that members of organizations are in for a grievous shock when the final evaluation takes place. I think they will discover that they have spent most of their energy on organizational and personal kingdom building.

Your comments about Martin Luther were helpful. Thank you.

I believe that God will ultimately be successful in influencing everyone's will for their own good and His glory. He will not force us against our will, He will just make us willing, then we will do the choosing. AND BELIEVE ME, HE KNOWS HOW TO PULL THE SWITCH AND MAKE US WILLING!!!

You put far too much value on free will – FAR TOO MUCH VALUE! With all due respect to your position under God, this is BAY FAR the strongest disagreement I have with you. Our action will always be a moral action for God will see to it that we will want to do His will. He will demonstrate to everyone experimentally that it is neither comfortable nor profitable to disregard His will. This is the only just and righteous way for God to conduct Himself. I apologize for the severity of my expression of disagreement to a man of such stature and caliber as you are, BUT I FEEL THIS POINT VERY STRONGLY!!

The doctrine of endless hell is so paralyzingly powerful that it never has to be mentioned, and still it will take the prominent place in the subconscious of the believer, and therefore it is indeed the major doctrine around which all others pivot. In its own quiet and powerful way it is the primary driving force behind most of the activities of those who believe it.

I would like to caution you about your conclusion that when God commands something we ought to be able to do it. Your almost glib use of this "logic" has certainly hurt me. I hope you have not hurt others too. You speak it so matter-of-factly, without allowing for other factors that might have some influence on the working out of this "logical conclusion."

Although I'm not able to believe many of the things that you folk do, I am very grateful for your expressions of love.

You are wrong about my never having faith, only hope. I do have faith in <u>my interpretation</u> of the Bible.

It's a comfort to me that you personally think that I belong to Jesus. That is indeed the way I want it to be.

You don't think that hell is as bad as a nervous breakdown; yet you strongly assert that you believe the Bible is the word of God. It is impossible for me to understand such a conclusion!

I am finding out experimentally that by rejecting your interpretation of scripture I am regaining joy and peace, and faith in the essential goodness of God; and I'm going to stick with what works for me.

I find great comfort in believing that GOD WAS THE AUTHOR OF MY TORTURE. Since it was not my choosing, I cannot help believing that God had a good reason for it.

You are wrong that I have nothing to base my faith on. I base it on <u>my</u> interpretation of scripture just as you base you faith on <u>your</u> interpretation of scripture.

Although I reject nearly everything you say, still I need and gladly accept the spirit of love and compassion in which you say it; for I recognize this as the very life-blood of the Holy Spirit of God.

I believe that God will do for others what He has done for me. Because of the torture He has allowed me to endure I no longer have a free will that is capable of rebelling against Him. My will has been sealed forever to do His will.

Rebelling against <u>your opinion</u> of what is God's will for me is quite a different matter however. I have had to reject your opinions to find peace and joy and faith, and I am grateful to God that He is giving me the power to reject your opinion of God's will for me.

God won't make people submit against their will; He will just make them willing to submit.

The rest of my life will prove that the suffering that God allowed me to experience has made it impossible for me to intentionally resist God's will. <u>No one</u> will ever choose to rebel against God once they have experienced what I have gone through!

I love you "T," and I desire only the very best for you and your group, but I regard your teachings to be error just as strongly as you do mine.

I believe that hell will convince every created being , including Satan, that rebellion is not worthwhile. It will effectively demonstrate the consequences of rebellion and change their minds about their rebellious attitude. It will be just as effective as my torture was for me.

Roger

Oswald Chambers says, "There are some types of suffering before which the only thing you can do is to keep your mouth shut. There are times when a man needs to be handled by God, not by his fellow men, and part of the gift of man's wisdom is to know how to be reverent with what he does not understand. The reason we are going through the things we are is that God wants to know whether He can make us good bread with which to feed others. The stuff of our lives, not simply our talk is to be the nutriment of those who know us."

"One of the greatest strains in life is the strain of waiting for God. 'Because thou didst keep the word of my patience.'" God takes the person like a bow which He stretches, and at a certain point the person says, "I can't stand it anymore." But God does not heed; He goes on stretching because He is aiming at His mark, not ours, and our patience is that we hang in there until God lets the arrow fly."

"If your hopes are being disappointed just now it means that they are being purified. There is nothing noble the human mind has ever hoped for or dreamed of that will not be fulfilled. Don't jump to conclusions too quickly; many things lie unsolved, and the biggest test of all is that God looks as if He were totally indifferent. Remain spiritually tenacious."

"The sphere of humiliation is always the place of more satisfaction to Jesus Christ. God wants us to live down in the valley at the drab commonplace pitch. We never live for the glory of God on the mount; we see His glory there, but it is in the valley that we live for the glory of God."

"Do we follow the Lamb withersoever He goeth? 'For the Lamb which is in the midst of the throne shall feed them and shall lead them unto living fountains of water, and God shall wipe away all tears from their eyes.'"

"When a word of God comes to a soul after a time of difficulty and perplexity, it is almost impossible to tell the ineffable sweetness of that word as it comes with the unction of the Holy Spirit!"

And now I would like to make some additional comments about the letter from "T".

He refers to those who refuse to yield to the drawing power of God's love. It's not saying much for the power of God's love when a created being of His is successfully able to seal himself into a never ending state of hell such as the Bible describes. I can readily see that God would use such a measure to cause His created beings to wise-up and learn that their rebellion is not worthwhile; but to say that anyone would actually choose to stay in such a state borders on the thinking of an insane sadist. To be able to believe such a thing is totally beyond my comprehension.

Because I love the two children that I helped create, I would do everything in my power – even inflict intense pain upon them for a limited period of time, to prevent them from having to experience the consequences of becoming a criminal. HOW MUCH MORE will God's love inflict pain if necessary, to prevent His created beings from having to be sealed forever into the state that the Bible describes as hell! It is my sincere hope that hell is part of the redemptive process, and although it may not be able to change anybody, it may cause them to come to the One who can change them.

There surely must be something wrong with a person's thinking process when they talk about how much God loves everyone, but they don't think He will use the severest of measures to convince His created beings that selfish rebellion is not worthwhile.

Ray Prinzing makes the following observation – "The radio preacher declares that man makes his choice, and once it is made, God cannot done thing about. He is saying that the will of man is more powerful than the will of God. It exalts the will of the creature above the will, purpose and plan of God. THE WORD OF GOD EXPOSES THIS AS BEING UTTERLY FALSE IN EVERY DEGREE."

An evangelical friend recently sent us an evangelical book on rearing children. The book tells of a nerve at the base of the neck which when squeezed causes intense pain. It recommends that this nerve be squeezed repeatedly until the desired obedience is obtained from the child; thus the child will learn for itself the consequence of not submitting to the one who is looking after them.

Will God do any less for his created creatures than we would do to obtain the desired results from those who are in our charge? And for the sake of those who already consider themselves to be children of God, I would like to point out that this method of neck squeezing works just as effectively on foster children and orphans as it does on our own children.

The letter writer "T" insists that the reason I don't have faith in the essential goodness of God is because I don't believe the Bible is the word of God, and since it's an incompatibility for God to command something and not give us the power to respond, he cannot believe that I have no faith, but rather that I'm not using the faith that he insists I have. My argument in return is that I can't exercise faith in a belief that's more incompatible with the justice and love of God than his illustration of incompatibility is.

He mentions two great forces, fear and faith. A greater force than both of these is love. By regarding my nervous breakdown an act of God's love I was able to recover from it. Had I kept attributing it to a second cause then in my thinking the second cause becomes greater than God and my fear promptly returns.

"T" once made the statement that his group didn't have time for nervous breakdowns. Listen friend – NOBODY TAKES TIME to have a nervous breakdown!

Evangelicals say that a God of <u>love</u> would never torture people to force them to change their mind, because that wouldn't be <u>love</u>. But instead they believe this same God of <u>love</u> is going to let them suffer endlessly in the place that the Bible graphically describes as hell. Their method of reasoning completely baffles me.

The insistence of "T" that I shouldn't equate my nervous breakdown with hell bears no weight as a reasonable argument. The language that the Bible uses to describe hell indicates that it must certainly be at least as bad as a nervous breakdown, but "T" does not seem to accept this part of the Bible as the reliable word of God. If he did he would believe it just the way it reads. It is my experience that evangelicals gloss over or explain away any of the passages of scripture that cause insurmountable problems when they try to believe them just the way they read.

I too believe that righteousness is by faith and not by self effort. But I cannot exercise faith in a god whose character is completely revolting. He will never be able to find a way into my mind using his concept of the character of God.

Faith is only stronger than fear when that faith is placed in an acceptable concept of God. Experience is showing me that hope in the total restoration concept of God is for me stronger than fear.

"T" says the reason I don't have faith is because I don't believe the Bible. This is not even an intelligent statement because in essence it is saying the reason I don't have faith is because I don't have faith! I DON'T WANT HIS KIND OF FAITH. I'd rather live out my life in hope than believe in a god who lets people suffer endlessly.

"T" says, "Faith is believing on the best evidence – the word of God. "But whose interpretation of the "word of God" – his?! When there's a choice, it makes more sense to choose the interpretation that glorifies the character of God the most. Punishing to reform glorifies God, but punishing endlessly with no good end in view does not glorify God at all!

"T" said, "God is going to have everything the way He wants it but I don't know what that means." It surely cannot mean that He <u>wants</u> anyone to suffer endlessly in a hell like the Bible describes. And it's my hope that if God doesn't want something to happen He can and will do something about it.

I wonder if "T" would still have the issue settled that God is love and just if God plunged him into the experience that I went through, where every effort to reach out to God and plead for mercy was only met by increased terror, week after week and month after month till I was on the brink of suicide. I'm sure his letter would be much different than the one he wrote, if indeed he was able to come out of it at all.

Job 12:16 says, "The deceived and the deceiver <u>are His</u>." Isaiah 66:4 says, "I will also choose their delusions and will bring their fears upon them."

What a relaxing thought it is to realize that it is God who chooses our delusions and brings our fears upon us! He knows exactly what we need to be believing at any given stage of our lives and He will allow us to stay in those deceptions only long enough to learn what He wants us to learn. It is my hope that God makes a plan for each life that He works out in response to our limited free will, and that this plan includes allowing us to stay in various deceptions for varying lengths of time to accomplish a good purpose.

God has allowed me to have hope that He is in charge of any deception I might be involved in, and that He will bring me to a triumphant conclusion, not just in spite of my deception, but rather by using it to do a work in me. I hope that this is what God is really like!

Although I shall always love the evangelicals, for the sake of my sanity and my emotional well being, I must totally and completely reject much of what they teach.

The next letter writer was a good friend of mine until his concept of God got in the way of our friendship. After listening to me bare my soul in a seven hour conversation he came to two conclusions. One, that I was not the person he thought I was; and two, that it was entirely possible that he would have to stand at the judgment and say, "I told you so" as God banished me to hell.

Here is the first of his two letters to me:

Dear Roger:

Peace! Peace, in Jesus' name. Be still and calm in Jesus' name, the name which is above every name and to which every knee shall bow and every tongue shall confess, of things in heaven, things in earth, and things under the earth that He is LORD, to the glory of God the Father.

Why should I begin like this? Roger, there is great compassion in my heart for you. I can truly say that God has not just given me a sympathetic heart for you, but one of compassion and love in Christ. You need HIS peace. I bring that to you in this letter in the name of Jesus.

I do not write with any condemnation in my heart. I have poured out my heart to God for you more than once. There has been strong agony in prayer. I have prayed earnestly for you. I can say that only once or twice before in my Christian life have I experienced such a moving of the Holy Spirit on my being to pray for someone. I can truly say that God is working for you and in your behalf.

We have expressed our feelings regarding our friendship. I am writing so that you may read this over and over and over again if you wish. We are your friends. I am your friend. This is our choice and we also believe that God has given us hearts of love for you; not just natural love – His love. The kind of love that goes beyond even our natural ability to love. We thank HIM for this. We are glad that this is HIS desire for you.

Have I read your letter? Yes. I have read it and reread it. I am very sorry that your preoccupation with the doctrine of judgment in the end times seems to have robbed you of your ability to see evidences of God's love for you.

May I share with you the positive, concrete things that I believe to be more important to your welfare than anything else. (May I interject here that I do not believe that your problem is a doctrinal one.)

Here are the steps to your deliverance:

1. Healing – memory, physical body, emotions, mind (rethinking past events,) and fears (controllable and uncontrollable.)

2. Time – Helen needs to be alive for at least 10 years so I will be able to cope with life if she were not here.

3. Attitudes – the attitudes of those who oppose me need to be changed to accept me as I am.

4. Commitments – I will commit my friends to God.

5. Future – to have a ministry of some kind to help those that have had the same problems that I have had.

Editor's note: "D" gleaned these points from me during our seven hour conversation.

Roger, please re-read the first two paragraphs at this point. Thank you.

Roger, I am praying in Jesus' Name, that more than anything you will have a sound mind.

If any of us are to be pleasing to God and have a Spirit anointed ministry we must be delivered from our worst enemy, ourselves.

I sense that I should stop writing at this point.

Roger, I would like to say that I am available to help you. I am praying for you. I have asked specific prayer for you. I have asked people to pray with an unprejudiced mind. I believe that they are. If you will be as unprejudiced in your mind about receiving the help and love that God brings to you, I am sure that your deliverance need not be a long drawn-out conflict.

I personally have never seen so many people in one place that express God's love as here in our group. Do they have problems? Sure they do. Do they make mistakes? Sure they do. Do they loveGod and want to do what's right? A loud YES. Can they forgive and forget? A louder YES. Can you? A louder YES.

I'm sure that anyone here that has had any problem with you would be willing to forgive and forget if they really knew there was a problem. Give them a chance that you want and I'm sure they will give you back just as much love, respect and confidence in you that I really believe they have had in you.

Peace, in Jesus' Name. God bless you. I'm available.

Greet Helen and the kids. We love you all, and we all love you.

> "D"

I appreciate the fact that "D" became very much involved in my problem.

However he cannot accept the fact that I am finding deliverance by rejecting his concept of God. This becomes even more evident his next letter to me. Even though he read A DESERT JOURNEY twice, he ignored the several times I expressed a measure of deliverance, and he wrote to me as though I still had the weight of the whole problem upon me.

When he says, "Your problem is not doctrinal but sometimes we are our own worst enemy," he is referring to the opinion of his group that a crises experience of "sanctification" causes us to "die to self." He has concluded on the basis of the evidence available to him that I am not "dead to self." Whether I am or not I am content to leave up to God. I don't think it's always possible to determine by outward manifestations if a person is really dead to self. However, since "D" has taken the liberty of arriving at a conclusion based on outward evidence, I would like to take the liberty of saying something that has bothered me for many years.

I lived hour after hour and day after day with the group that "D" belongs to. I worked with them, ate with them, shared living quarters with them, and overheard many of their conversations during a period of more than three years. On the basis of outward manifestations it was my observation that not one single person was "dead to self." Yet everyone claimed to have had an experience called "sanctification" after which they were supposed to be "dead to self." Some were a lot more dead than others.

I remember the day in 1961 that my former pastor stood in the chapel and announced that the assistance pastor and he decided together that if anyone had not had the experience of the crises called "sanctification," then they were not really dead to self.

One staff member actually said, (and they were serious), that unless a person had had the experience of sanctification they wouldn't even go to heaven. Yet it was my observation that nobody in that group was "dead to self."

Ray Prinzing believes the Bible teaches that both the "new birth" and "sanctification" are processes. I hope for my sake that he's right. I'll explain why later on.

One teacher told us that even if we lived a Godly life until we grew old, but then under torture we renounced Christ, we would go to endless hell.

In the pages ahead there will be many illustrations that will show that the basic motivating force of the evangelical system is FEAR. I will show that fear permeates every area of their thinking and conduct. When one is in the process of leaving the system as I am, one has the unique opportunity of finding out things that could never be found out by those who remain loyal subjects of their evangelical kingdom.

The following is my reply to the letter from "D." Most of the statements are grossly exaggerated, if not out-right lies. I don't believe I have ever had true faith, maybe just a little but not much. Upon rewriting this letter years later, my hope has become strong enough to face up to the fact that I was pretending to have a lot more than I really had, or even have now.

I lied to "D" for the same reason that I lied to "T" – because I was afraid. Most of the things I said was just wishful thinking and not reality at all.

I lied because I could sense that the most precious thing in my life was being challenged – my HOPE; and it was being challenged by a friend to whom I had bared my soul for seven hours. I lied because I could not, and still cannot emotionally cope with evangelicals.

Here then, for what its worth, (not much,) is my reply to "D's" first letter:

Dear "D":

Thank you for your letter.

Something good has happened to me. Faith and joy have returned to my life.

I am grateful for the deep concern you have been feeling for me. God has been hearing your prayers and feeling your concern with you and has ministered to my need.

I was deeply disappointed to find out that you consider it possible that you might have to stand at the judgment and say, "I tried to tell you so" as you watch me being banished to hell. However, I am no longer overwhelmed by the opinions of evangelicals like I used to be.

If my uncontrollable fear feelings continue to dissipate at the same rate that they have over the past few weeks, by the time we come there on vacation they should be completely gone.

My fear feelings began to dissipate rapidly right after I listened to Ray Prinzing's cassette KEPT IN PEACE and read

Hannah Hurnard's THE SECRET OF A TRANSFORMED LIFE.

God has granted me the power to forgive my evangelical friends who have come to the wrong conclusion about me and my former problem. He has also granted me the power to neutralize the negative power of the influence that evangelicals had on my life. Also He has granted me the solid confidence in the total restoration of everyone, a confidence that I have been wanting for a long time.

"D," my problem was doctrinal. I think what you may have to do is ask God for grace to accept the fact that He blesses even people like me who believe things that you consider to be heresy.

You will think that I've been delivered in spite of my beliefs. But I know that I have been delivered because I rejected your beliefs and embraced a new set of beliefs that glorifies God more.

Anyway, let us rejoice together that I have indeed been delivered.

> Roger

The following letter from "D" hurt me very much, which clearly showed me that there wasn't much reality to my grand claims of "deliverance" in my letter to him.

His letter is a good example of what evangelicals really think of me when they are not trying to spare my feelings.

Dear Roger:

There are many things that I praise God for each day. I am glad that I can, and have for some time been giving Him praise and glory for the work of grace and mercy that He is doing in your heart. I recognize that it is a work that <u>He</u> is doing and not me or you. Praise His name.

I am sorry that I cannot accept doctrines like the ones you have accepted because they are not based on <u>all</u> of scripture. <u>All</u> scripture is given by inspiration of God and is profitable for doctrine, for correction, for instruction in righteousness, and for reproof. II Timothy 3:16.

I would like to come to you not with man's wisdom, but in demonstration of the Spirit and power.

It is too bad that you think you know more about what I think than I do. I know this will come hard and coarse to you. So be it. The problem is not that you are right or that I am right. Let <u>God</u> be true and every man a liar. Much of your talk has been just that.

It is interesting that you should think I have a small concept of God. Maybe I do – but are you not becoming a judge?

I would not be quick to say you have been delivered in the sense that the scripture speaks of deliverance. If you have been, praise God. I am only concerned for your best eternal good – not just your happiness and peace of mind in this life only.

I am being bold to speak so sharp and strong Roger, because I know that the center of my motive is God's love for you.

I see logic problems in your thinking. I see legal (moral government of God) problems in your thinking.

I'm not saying that I have arrived and that you have not, that I am right and you are not; but I am saying that God is right and the only one who can justify and make sinners (people who do and think wrong) righteous, and He receives all the glory.

Certainly I cannot take the space in letter form to point out what the scriptures say. I am not even sure at this point that you accept the total inspiration of the scriptures. If you do not, that is too bad for you. It does not make them any less inspired because you do not believe it.

Well, I trust you will receive what I have said in the same spirit of love and concern that it has been written.

"D"

Dear "D"

Thank you for your letter. Thank you also that the center of your motive is God's love for me.

I cast myself and my beliefs on God. He will take care of me. Of this I am more certain than about anything else. <u>He</u> is the One who put me through torture, and He is the One who has now brought faith, peace and joy to my heart.

The judgment of Christ will reveal just how much of my talk is lies and how much is truth. I'm content to leave it at that. To the best of my knowledge I have spoken no lies.

I cannot emotionally cope with coming to visit you on vacation now that I have experienced the pain that your last letter caused me.

Roger

I, Roger Tutt, have never had assurance of salvation. I have never had the witness of the Holy Spirit that I'm a child of God. In an effort to convince myself that I did have these things I pretended that I had them. I carried on this pretense for 28 years. By pretending, I hoped that I could convince myself and others that it was true. My pretense finally caught up to me and caused a complete nervous breakdown.

Evangelicals say, "If you're saved, you know it; if you don't know it you're not." According to evangelical theology, I, Roger Tutt am destined to spend eternity in hell.

Recently, God has granted me hope – hope that the evangelicals are wrong. The main theme of the rest of my book will expound the reasons why I feel justified in rejecting evangelicalism and placing my hope in a different concept of God.

My feelings of security regarding life after death depend on evangelicalism being wrong. My only hope is that hell for me will come to an end FOR I CANNOT LOVE OR TRUST A GOD WHO ALLOWS HIS CREATED BEINGS TO SUFFER ENDLESSLY.

Total restoration is not an optional point of view. It's the very essence of the reason why I want to go on living. It's the only thing that really matters in my life.

Evangelicalism has become my arch-enemy – infinitely more powerful in a negative way than Satan himself.

I suffer a high degree of emotional pain when I attempt to fellowship with evangelicals on a social level. I cannot foresee that I shall ever be able to enjoy their pretense again.

I no longer consider "D" a friend, for he attacked the most precious and only really important thing in my life – my HOPE.

After the emotional pain subsided, I made the following comments on his letter:

It wasn't so very long ago that a letter like his may have caused my suicide. In his letter he came to me in the power of the spirit of his group, not in a demonstration of the Holy Spirit and power.

As far as "D" is concerned, his group doesn't have just an interpretation of the word of God – their beliefs are the very word of God itself.

What "D" calls "just words" is the most precious thing in my life. I cannot emotionally cope with a person who calls my hopes "just words." They frighten me too much. I have to leave them alone – let them go their way and I'll go mine. They don't just make me uncomfortable – they cause me a high degree of emotional pain. I'm sorry, but that's the way it is. And until God grants me faith I don't foresee that there will be any change.

I believe the Bible only contains the word of God. I agree with the old American Standard translators who translated Timothy's verse, "All scripture <u>that is inspired by God</u> is profitable . . ." Although I have read several evangelical books that were supposed to prove the canonicity and infallibility of scripture and also taken a Bible school course on the subject – I still think that Bible only contains the word of God. Believing that the Bible is infallible and authoritative has caused an immeasurable amount of harm. MY ability to be free to question the infallibility of scripture is one of the greatest gifts that God has given me, and I thank Him for it.

"D" condemns me for becoming a judge as to whether or not he has a poorer concept of God than I. I know the scripture says, "Judge not lest ye be judged." But I sure don't mind being judged for thinking I have a better concept of God than he. The fact is that my concept is <u>infinitely</u> better than his!

"D" was right about my not having been "delivered." Until I can emotionally cope with people like him I cannot rightly claim to have been "delivered" from the bondage to fear that evangelicalism produces in me. Spiritually I am floundering badly. I need God to strengthen my hope.

Several of my friends, including my wife who is my best friend, have been urging me to make a clean break from the evangelicals. I am gradually becoming more and more free from their bondage.

None of the "hopes" in my statement of hope are "just words" to me. Ray Prinzing phrased it well in a recent letter to me. He said, "We praise God for these truths, they are far more than just a mere form of head knowledge because He causes the Word to become life within, and then He works it out by experience through the various processings of the day. Nor would we seek to escape any of those processings either, for the challenge of the overcomer remains high in our vision. But we would sink our roots ever deeper into Christ, and draw from Him that strength sufficient for the day."

My evangelical friends tell me that they love me and that I should forget everything else. This I cannot do. My hope in total restoration is too important to me. It is more precious to me than my life. I would rather die than lose my hope. It's really the only thing that matters to me anymore. It brought me back from hell and because of it I am beginning to really enjoy life for the first time. Because my hope in total restoration means so much to me I intend to do my very best to defend this hope in the following pages of my book.

During my years of Bible school in the States, I developed a close friendship with another Canadian student who later married my wife's sister. After I was dismissed from the missionary society under which I had served for seven years, my Canadian friend asked me if my primary concern in seeking another job was "ministry or money." Now that I am leaving evangelicalism, he is probably glad that I don't have more of a "ministry" than I do!

I introduce my Canadian friend because today we received a letter from his wife. Although she is also an evangelical she is able to identify with me because she suffered in a similar manner.

Dear Roger:

I guess I never wrote you after you sent your DESERT JOURNEY. I jotted down a number of points where I could say I really knew what he felt about other people's reactions.

The difficulties I had during our first five years here in Brazil, and the dark time I went through taught me that there are times when one doesn't give lots of ideas and advice to another. The soul goes through times that cannot be understood by others, and I know what human counsel and advice sounds and feels like during that time – however well meaning it may be. It's rather like sand in a wound.

It's better to say, "I don't know the answer to your questions, but I'll pray that God sends you someone with more understanding than I have, who <u>can</u> help." And that is, and has been my attitude.

The more I read, the more I see how many people struggle with the most perplexing questions.

I trust that God is enabling you to find more answers, Roger. Every time I am reminded of you, I pray that the Holy Spirit will minister the deep comfort and peace that is His – and continue to do so.

Love

Joan

How can people as nice as this letter writer believe so insanely? How can these evangelicals believe it is just and good for God to create beings who will want, or at least have to suffer torment endlessly. It's the fact that they are so kind and loving that has made it even more difficult to break away from them. If they were obnoxious it would be easy for me to escape from their influence, but most of the time they are as nice as anybody could reasonably expect them to be.

Surely it must be the greatness of the grace of God that by-passes their beliefs and governs their hearts in spite of their insane thinking. It took me a long time to realize that they are not nice people because of what they believe but they are nice people BY THE GRACE OF GOD ALONE. When I began to see this I was able to begin breaking away from their tyrannical system that kept me so long in bondage to fear.

In the pages ahead, I am going to discuss at some length the differences between the evangelical concept of God and the total restorationist concept of God. And I intend to show how and why evangelicalism is losing its credibility and its power over my soul.

# VACATION 1976

As I said before, attempting to socialize with evangelicals causes me a high degree of emotional pain. Because of this I didn't go on vacation with my wife and children this year.

My wife is able to feel comfortable with evangelicals because God has granted her <u>faith</u> in total restoration, whereas He has only granted me <u>hope</u>.

The following are excerpts from the letters we exchanged during the weeks she was gone from me:

Dear Roger:

I think that you could come and be comfortable here. Only your coming will ever prove it, but knowing your problem as I do, I really think you would have no problem with people – only with things you think about like having a good time, etc.

Also I feel that it would do no good and probably a lot of damage to send your new manuscript because you would be making problems where there aren't any. I have an idea that they might all say they don't have time and don't want to hear about it because they like and accept you for what you are now rather than what you were ten years ago. They don't have a need to know everything you think before they like and accept you. Just like you wish they thought like you, they wish you thought like them; but being that you don't and they don't, your basic destination is the same. They are taken up more now with living than with brimstone.

I don't say, "Don't sent it," I'm just saying what I think at this time.

I feel that these people really don't get concerned or upset with a different point of view as long as the person loves the Lord. To tell you the truth, they don't have time. I think that whoever you send the new book to will feel that if it is more of the same as the first, they won't want to take the time to read it because if you don't agree with them that's your business.

They still like you for you, not for believing what they do. Granted, they would like it if everyone believed the same as them, but I think they have realized that everyone who loves the Lord doesn't. From the feel I get from the place as a whole, it would just make problems for the ones who are the most conscientious, and the ones who aren't wouldn't be phased by it, - as far as changing anyway.

You wanted my honest opinion and I'm afraid you will think I am being influenced by them because I talk as though there is no problem. There is a problem as far as people's beliefs go, but I don't think there is a problem for you coming here, because people aren't expecting anything – just you to be you.

You have to accept them as them and let their problems be theirs' and Gods' – not take on their problems for them because they don't seem to be living the way they should – believing as they do.

We want them to accept us and not want us to change so they can like us, so we have to do the same! They are doing what <u>they</u> feel God wants <u>them</u> to do and believe, so we have to let them. If God wants it changed it's up to Him. We have to feel just as accepting of them regardless of if they change.

We feel that what we are doing and believing is right for us, and so do they. We have to accept that God is leading them a different way, just as He is leading us. If He weren't, neither us nor they would be where we are.

If we really believe that God is working <u>all</u> things after His own plan, then we can relax and enjoy His people in whatever stage he has them in.

We can't be anyone else's conscience, and unless God speaks about things that bother you and me – about what to do or believe, then it's none of our business to act as the Holy Spirit. I say this because I don't think I would like it if they started writing to us saying we should stop drinking and smoking because they felt it was wrong. I think you would feel too that – what business is that of yours?!

I know that you are probably disappointed that I am not standing up and fighting so to speak, but there is nothing to fight. This group is not the small picky fellowship that it used to be – unless you snoop around and pick up all the little things here and there.

After being here awhile I can see why "D" said he thought this place was OK, because everyone is so busy with their own department and private lives that they don't have time for trivial things like – people getting upset with people.

Humans are humans and it's between them and the Lord they way things work out, not to us looking in. We have to leave the "whys" and "if that's the way thens" up to the Lord.

After I had been here awhile I laughed a crying sort of disappointed sarcastic laugh, because you could have come this year with no problem or uncomfortableness with anyone – on their side of things. The problem lies with you not being able to feel comfortable because you wish they didn't believe the way they do. I can see you have a real problem if all the things you are writing about bother you enough to be uncomfortable when you are with them.

To look as it from their standpoint, they probably wish that you could be as comfortable with what they think as they are with what you think. They probably think, "Why can't he accept us for us regardless of how we think, and leave everything up to God?"

I guess when you count all the bad things that happen as areas where God will make it better that it happened that way with them, this could be an area. If we really believe God is going to bring everyone to Himself then that means people who have a wrong concept of Him too. We should be happy for how much He has been able to do rather than concentrating on what there is left to do.

Mom said today that she knows <u>someday</u> you'll be able to come back. She wishes it were now, but she knows you will be stronger and freer after you get done writing and things get more settled.

Sure wish you could meet us at the cabins. You get off on Friday night and could get there by Saturday night. I'll send you the address and how to get there. Wow! Would that be a surprise for the kids and everyone else. I sure talk like you're coming don't I! Guess I kind of like having you around.

I probably made everything sound too simple like there's nothing wrong here. I didn't mean to. There certainly are people who would be ready to try to change your mind or point out your errors, but I don't think you would have much to do with them even if we knew who they were. The ones with whom you have to do accept you for you and don't have any desire to try to change or convert you to their way of thinking.

For you own good I think you need to write the things you are writing, and it could well be for your own good you will need to send it to the same people you sent A DESERT JOURNEY to. I don't know, but I want you to do what you need to do.

We love you lots!

Helen, Steve and Beth

Before I record more excerpts from my wife's letters I would like to insert some excerpts from my letters to her. Because I have no faith – only hope, I suffer a high degree of emotional pain when attempting to socialize with evangelicals who have a theology with which I cannot emotionally cope. Helen did not yet understand this fact when she wrote to me.

Dear Helen:

I love you very much!

Thanks for being so understanding in the past. I have been so grateful for it. I am asking you now to exercise just a little more understanding and try not to be too much hurt by what I am going to say.

Your efforts to try to get me to come there have caused me some unhappiness. I'm sorry to make you sad by not coming but without faith I just cannot emotionally cope. Staying home alone is the lesser of two not nice things. When you read my book you will understand better.

I'm sorry Helen. Please stick with me. Please try to understand. Please realize that I may never be able to visit there again. It hurt so much when you tried to change my mind about coming.

Give me time. Give me lots of time. Give me years if necessary – lots of years if necessary.

Our chorus director's wife attempted suicide. It could have been me on any given day during the past ten years. Only the hope that I have is sustaining me – a hope that is contrary to what our evangelical friends have faith in.

Helen, once you read my book I think you will change your mind about it doing more harm than good.

Thanks so much for your phone call. The best thing you said was that you're still lonely even with all the people around there. I'm still glowing over that statement! THANKS!!

I love you so very much!

Roger

Dear Roger:

It was really good to talk to you yesterday. I felt bad that I had made you feel bad when talking about coming to visit here. I don't care if you never come back as long as you stay well.

You're better now than you have ever been, so I'd rather you stayed like that than to become sick just to spend a couple of weeks somewhere. You might not get sick visiting, but you wouldn't be very relaxed or comfortable. I think it would help to have more time between too.

I probably wouldn't feel as comfortable if I hadn't grown up here. When a person knows so many people it's easier to find someone whom you feel more comfortable with.

I love you very much Roger. I marvel at how you keep so honest and go through so many things and stay loving.

Did I tell you that I went up to Mom and Dad's after the kids were in bed Sunday night and had a visit? We didn't talk very much about doctrine except I said that it has helped you and you Dad so much that I wouldn't knock it. I said I saw a lot of good in it, and the view of God is so big that it is terrific!

I love you Roger.

Helen

After my family returned home from vacation I sent the following letter to several of our evangelical friends:

Dear Friends:

I would like to comment on a few of the things that Helen has told me you have said.

Firstly you ask, "What does Roger think he can say that would stop us from liking him?"

More than several times in the past I have heard you folk say, "What that person needs is to get saved." After you read my book my concern will not be that you will stop liking me, but rather that you will not consider me saved – in your definition of the word. Since I have no faith I cannot emotionally cope with visiting you knowing that you believe I need to "get saved."

Secondly you ask, "Why does he keep writing like he's trying to pick a fight with us?"

After you read my book you will understand that I'm not "trying to pick a fight with you." It will explain so many things that you don't yet understand about me.

Helen says that when you said, "We love you – forget the rest," you meant that what I believe is not a problem to you. Maybe it isn't, but what you believe is a VERY BIG PROBLEM to me. And because you love me and want to try to understand me I want you to read my book.

Keep in mind that it is not my purpose to hurt anybody. If I didn't believe that you loved me and wanted to try to understand me, I wouldn't bother to send you my book – I would just simply never visit you again. Unless God grants me faith I won't ever be able to visit you again – even if you do read my book.

Although I find it emotionally impossible to cope with the way you believe, I do love you and I don't want to hurt you for any reason. Although the contents of the book may cause you some hurt, it will help you to understand why I cannot enjoy your company.

A good illustration of my problem about coming there can be made by calling to your remembrance the time when "L" was speaking out strongly against the Roman Catholics in one of his conference sermons. A man got up in the middle of his sermon, walked to the back and called out, "Excuse me a moment. I want you to know that I'm a Roman Catholic and I came here today" – and then he walked out.

When I visit with you nearly everything you say is said in a know-it-all – we have all the answers – way, that it offends me and causes me no small degree of emotional suffering.

Thank you for helping my family have a good time. You have always been real good at that.

Roger

Here is a note from my wife's mother:

Dear Roger:

How wonderful for all the bitterness to be gone from your heart. There must have been many hurts, wounds, etc., over the years. How did you get rid of it all?

I know from experience that resentment, whether it is open or pushed down so I am scarcely aware of it, leads me to a lot of trouble. It eats the heart out of me, turns things sour and leads to bitterness.

I trust you will take these remarks as something shared and not that I think I have the last word on the subject. OK? I have lots to learn.

Are you having your book typed up now Roger? We will be waiting.

God bless you all.

Love – Mom

Dear Mom:

Thanks for your letter.

The hope produced in my spirit as I read THE SECRET OF A TRANSFORMED LIFE by Hannah Hurnard and listened to a cassette called KEPT IN PEACE by Ray Prinzing – this "hope" dislodged the bitterness I had in my heart towards evangelicals.

Editor's note: This "hope" is not strong enough, however, to prevent me from suffering a high degree of emotional pain when I try to function with evangelicals on a social level.

Letter to Mom continued:

I don't generally read [you magazine] because I regard it to be based on a false foundation, (that is a wrong basic concept of God's character), and although there is much good in it, it has the same effect on me as reading the WATCHTOWER or THE PLAIN TRUTH would have on you. They also have much good in them.

However I did glance through your magazine this time, and because you had talked about resentment I was attracted to the article on healings and attitudes.

The psychologist that "T" referred to has a different definition of resentment than Webster. Webster says that resentment is simply, "a feeling of displeasure from a sense of being offended."

I've never heard of "T's" definition of resentment before. I agree that – "attempting to excuse our own failures by attributing them to injustice at the hands of some else" is certainly wrong and can lead, as he says to "self pity, emotional agony which seeks relief through the sympathy of others, hatred, vengeance, murder and insanity."

I would like for a moment to examine my own personal resentment in the light of "T's" definition.

It is true that I consider myself to have suffered injustice due to the misunderstandings and wrong conclusions that you folk and others maintain towards me, but I don't think I use it as an excuse for my own failures.

I suppose evangelicals might consider my book an attempt to seek relief through the sympathy of others, but I'm hoping that after they read it they will change their mind. Although they can't accept it, the fact is that I am finding relief by rejecting much of what evangelicalism teaches.

Any self pity, hatred, vengeance or murder that might be in my heart is being dislodged by my hope that evangelicals are wrong about many things.

The "insanity" that I experienced was caused by my reaction to the insistence of evangelicals that their concept of God was true. It wasn't caused so much by resentment as it was by the fact that for 28 years I had so completely committed myself to trying to embrace evangelicalism that it has been psychologically difficult for me to break away from their influence. I kept thinking to myself that if the evangelical concept of God is the true one, then I'd better be very careful about allowing any other concept take its place. Evangelicalism held me in bondage by fear.

It was not until I began breaking away from evangelicalism that I began to find release from bitterness, etc.

In your letter I assume you were referring to "T's" definition of resentment – not Webster's

Even if my book does nothing to change your attitude towards me, it will give me satisfaction to know that I did try my best to establish an understanding between us.

Love –

> Roger

It used to bother me that I might wind up as one of the oft used negative illustrations in the magazine or classroom of the missionary training center from which I graduated.

I think it would be unfortunate it they use me as an illustration of "one who started well but it not finishing well" as they used to like to put it.

From my point of view I have only just recently started to LIVE, and there has been nothing but positive results from rejecting much of what they teach.

"This book is the first in a series of a body of work which includes more than 3000 pages."

# About the Author

*Rodger Tutt is the Pen name for Ted Jones*

The idea that God lets any creature suffer endlessly has caused me more suffering than all other problems of my life combined. By the time I had reached the mission field I had hoped to have found a satisfactory answer that would justify God allowing this to happen. I didn't find such an answer. Surrounded by thousands of people, dozens of whom were dying every day and beginning an eternity of suffering in hell was too much for me.

In 1966, at age 28, it caused me to have a nervous breakdown. For several weeks I was confined to my bed in a state of terror night and day. The terror was caused by the fear of what a God I could not love or respect would do to me after I died. It took me twelve years to fully recover from the breakdown. I quickly became agnostic, for the Christian gospel and the Bible were no longer any comfort to me at all. Many evangelical friends tried to help me. They meant well, but in the end they all had only words of condemnation towards me. This added more suffering to my already intense suffering.

Gradually I began to learn that there have been, in centuries past, and still are today, a few people in the world that see a different kind of God in the Bible. They see a God who will not let any creature suffer forever. They see a God in the Bible who will change every second of everyone's suffering into something better that it happened, including the sufferings of Satan. I read dozens of books, and listened to hundreds of tapes by men who believe this way and I gradually became converted to believing this way myself.

Since 1981, through my newspaper ads and my telephone ministry, I have sent out many hundreds of packets of literature explaining why I believe as I do. I have also sent this evidence to hundreds of pastors and Bible school teachers. None of them have told me that they are able to refute it. I have also read eight books that were supposed to refute the evidence in favor of universalism, but none of them do. Because of this evidence, my panic attacks became less frequent until twelve years after my breakdown they ceased altogether. Now nothing gives me greater pleasure than to make this evidence available to others who have suffered because of the same problem I had, and I use a substantial amount of my money and time to this end.

Because of the enormous amount of suffering the idea of "endless hell" causes in this world, I am asking you to consider the possibility that you should stop endorsing the idea that the Bible teaches it. Or, at least, let others know that there are (and have been in centuries past) people who do not think the Bible teaches it.

Many of the responses from pastors and teachers range from a mild: "The majority don't agree with you so you must be wrong", to the vicious "For every week you leave your ad in the papers, God will increase the temperature of the fires of hell for you personally".

Most are somewhere in between these remarks. But none have told me they are able to refute the evidence. And, until they can, they will not be able to shut me up.

May God's blessing rest with your spirit!

Rodger Tutt

# Social Media links

Websites

http://hell-is-not-endless.com/

http://greater-emmanuel.org/Hope4You/

Facebook

https://www.facebook.com/ted.jones.73157203

Search the internet for "Rodger Tutt – Hell is not endless"
to find numerous conversations Ted has had on various
Christian forums and Web Pages.

56653963R00104

Made in the USA
Middletown, DE
24 July 2019